Did You Know?
Dinosaur

D1408225

SMITHSONIAN
INSTITUTION

Established in 1846, the Smithsonian Institution—the world's largest museum and research complex—includes 19 museums and galleries and the National Zoological Park. The total number of artifacts, works of art, and specimens in the Smithsonian's collection is estimated at 137 million, the bulk of which is contained in the National Museum of Natural History, which holds more than 126 million specimens and objects. The Smithsonian is a renowned research center, dedicated to public education, national service, and scholarship in the arts, sciences, and history.

DK SMITHSONIAN

Did You Know?
Dinosaur

Nicholas St. Fleur

Author Nicholas St. Fleur
Consultant Emily Keeble
Smithsonian consultant Matthew T. Miller,
Museum Specialist, Department of Paleobiology,
National Museum of Natural History, Smithsonian
Illustrators Dan Crisp, Arran Lewis, Ed Merritt

DK LONDON
Editor Sally Beets
Senior designer Ann Cannings
US Senior editor Shannon Beatty
US Editor Elizabeth Searcy
Additional editing Olivia Stanford, Lizzie Davey,
Jolyon Goddard, Katie Lawrence
Managing editors Laura Gilbert, Jonathan Melmoth
Managing art editor Diane Peyton Jones
Preproduction producer Dragana Puvacic
Producer Barbara Ossowska
Jacket designer Rachael Parfitt Hunt
Jacket coordinator Issy Walsh
Creative director Helen Senior
Publishing director Sarah Larter

DK DELHI
Designers Nidhi Mehra, Jaileen Kaur,
Nehal Verma, Seepiya Sahni
Editors Bharti Bedi, Radhika Haswani, Mark Silas
Managing editor Alka Thakur Hazarika
Managing art editor Romi Chakraborty
DTP designers Dheeraj Singh, Jagtar Singh,
Vijay Kandwal
CTS manager Balwant Singh
Production manager Pankaj Sharma
Project picture researcher Sakshi Saluja
Delhi team head Malavika Talukder

First American Edition, 2020
Published in the United States by
DK Publishing, 1450 Broadway, Suite 801,
New York, NY 10018

Contents

The age of the dinosaurs

Dinosaur anatomy

Find out whether I'm a dinosaur on page 124.

Senses and behavior

Dinosaur discovery

The end of the dinosaurs

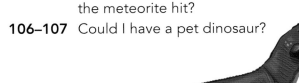

Find out whether you could keep me as a pet on page 106.

? Quick quiz

Test your knowledge! Look out for the "quick quiz" box throughout this book to see how much you've learned. You'll find some of the answers on the pages, but you may have to look up others or give your best guess. Turn to pages 130–131 for the answers.

The age of the dinosaurs

For more than 180 million years, the world belonged to the dinosaurs. Sharp-toothed Cryolophosaurus hunted small animals in forests, while Parasaurolophus looked for leafy greens. Mammals lived in the dinosaurs' shadows.

What is a dinosaur?

Dinosaurs were prehistoric reptiles that lived millions of years ago. You might have heard of the meat-eating Tyrannosaurus rex or the long-necked Diplodocus. Dinosaurs have many things in common, including legs positioned directly under their bodies, and laying and hatching from eggs.

Terrible lizard

In 1842, the English scientist Richard Owen gave a family of fossilized bones the name "Dinosauria," which comes from the Greek for "terrible lizard."

How do reptiles stand?

Lizard
Lizards have legs that spread out and away from their bodies. They move from side to side when they run.

Crocodile
Alligators and crocodiles are more upright than lizards. They wiggle their hips as they move.

Dinosaur
Dinosaurs had legs positioned directly under their bodies. This allowed them to run faster than modern reptiles.

 Quick quiz

1. What feature do all dinosaurs share?

2. Who was the scientist who gave the fossilized bones the name "Dinosauria"?

3. What does the name "Tyrannosaurus rex" mean?

See pages 130–131 for the answers.

How long ago did dinosaurs live?

Dinosaurs evolved 233 million years ago, or MYA, during the Mesozoic era (252 to 66 million years ago). The Mesozoic era was made up of the Triassic, Jurassic, and Cretaceous periods.

Before dinosaurs

A four-legged reptile with a sail on its back called Dimetrodon was around before the dinosaurs. •••••↗

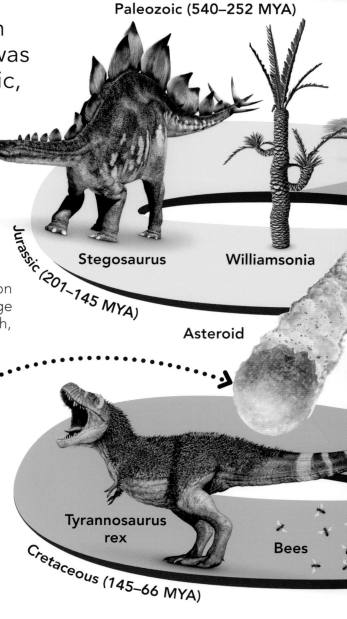

Dimetrodon   Glossopteris

Paleozoic (540–252 MYA)

Jurassic (201–145 MYA)

Stegosaurus   Williamsonia

Asteroid

Tyrannosaurus rex

Bees

Cretaceous (145–66 MYA)

What were the first dinosaurs to exist?

Herrerasaurus

One of the earliest known theropods, this sharp-toothed carnivore lived around 231 million years ago.

Eoraptor

Another early dinosaur, Eoraptor lived around 231 million years ago and was a quick, two-legged meat eater.

Extinction

Around 66 million years ago, a huge asteroid hit Earth, causing the extinction of the dinosaurs. •••

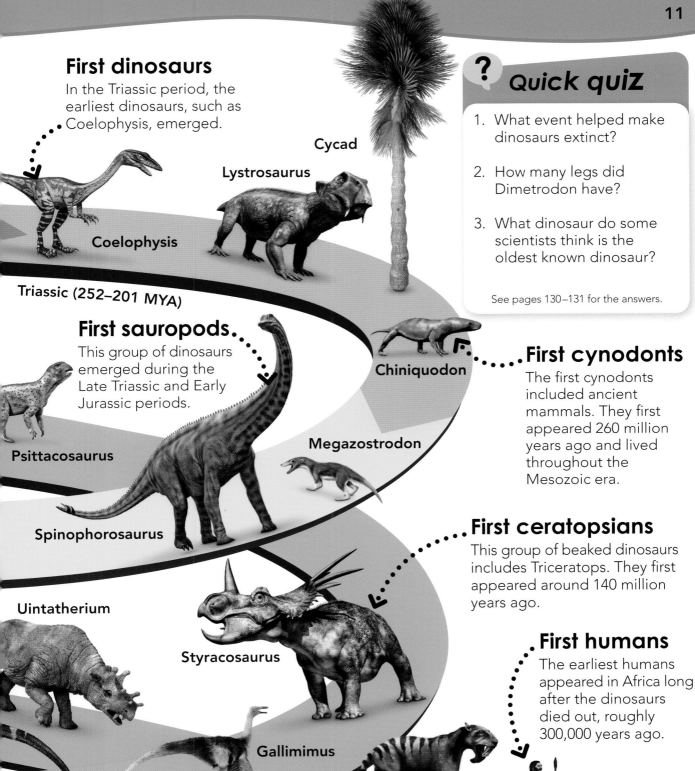

First dinosaurs

In the Triassic period, the earliest dinosaurs, such as Coelophysis, emerged.

Cycad

Lystrosaurus

Coelophysis

Triassic (252–201 MYA)

? Quick quiz

1. What event helped make dinosaurs extinct?

2. How many legs did Dimetrodon have?

3. What dinosaur do some scientists think is the oldest known dinosaur?

See pages 130–131 for the answers.

First sauropods

This group of dinosaurs emerged during the Late Triassic and Early Jurassic periods.

Chiniquodon

Psittacosaurus

Megazostrodon

First cynodonts

The first cynodonts included ancient mammals. They first appeared 260 million years ago and lived throughout the Mesozoic era.

Spinophorosaurus

First ceratopsians

This group of beaked dinosaurs includes Triceratops. They first appeared around 140 million years ago.

Uintatherium

Styracosaurus

First humans

The earliest humans appeared in Africa long after the dinosaurs died out, roughly 300,000 years ago.

Gallimimus

Thylacosmilus

Early human

Cenozoic (66 MYA to present)

Flowering plants

How has the world changed?

In prehistoric times, one huge mass of land, known as a supercontinent, existed on Earth. Over millions of years, it broke up and drifted apart. During this time, many types of animals evolved, including dinosaurs.

In the far future, today's continents will eventually drift together to form a new supercontinent.

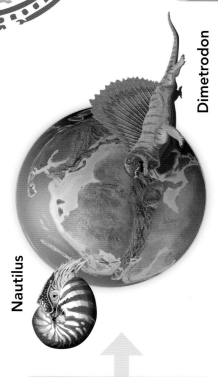

Nautilus

Dimetrodon

Isanosaurus

Plateosaurus

Permian
299–251 million years ago
During this period, there was just a single supercontinent called Pangaea. A group of mammal-like reptiles, including Dimetrodon, arose at this time. Dinosaurs had yet to emerge.

Triassic
252–201 million years ago
The first dinosaurs appeared in the middle of the Triassic era. Toward the end of this period, the Tethys Ocean began to split Pangaea into two vast continents.

? Quick quiz

1. Are the continents still moving?

2. What is the name of the supercontinent from the Permian period?

3. During what period did the dinosaurs go extinct?

See pages 130–131 for the answers.

Jurassic
201–145 million years ago
Pangaea had now broken up into two massive continents called Laurasia and Gondwana. The climate became warmer, and plants and dinosaurs flourished.

Kentrosaurus

Cryolophosaurus

Cretaceous
145–66 million years ago
In this period, the continents continued to move farther apart. T. rex lived during this time, but the Cretaceous period ended with the mass extinction of the dinosaurs.

Velociraptor

T. rex

Present day
Now, the world is divided into seven continents. Dinosaurs died out long ago, but their descendants—birds—still fly, run, and swim across the world.

Eagle

Human

Did dinosaurs change over time?

Early dinosaurs
The earliest dinosaur fossils are about 245 million years old. They belonged to small, agile reptiles that probably stood on two legs.

Later dinosaurs
Many differently shaped dinosaurs evolved from the early ones. Some were huge; some walked on four legs; and others had horns and body armor.

Where did dinosaurs live?

Dinosaurs lived all over the world. They evolved to call a wide variety of environments home, including rain forests, swamps, coastlines, plains, and deserts.

? *Quick quiz*

1. Did dinosaurs live in deserts?

2. Is the world the same now as when the dinosaurs were alive?

3. Did dinosaurs stay in the same areas?

See pages 130–131 for the answers.

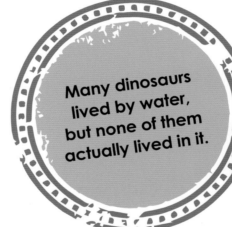

Many dinosaurs lived by water, but none of them actually lived in it.

Did dinosaurs move around?

Like many animals today, dinosaurs didn't stay put. They traveled across their world, often in search of food. For example, fossils show that huge sauropods, such as Camarasaurus, may have walked huge distances of hundreds of miles across North America.

Desert

Dry, dusty deserts were home to dinosaurs such as Velociraptor. They survived here despite frequent sandstorms.

Forest

Riverside forests were home to many dinosaurs. Cryolophosaurus hunted other dinosaurs that ate leaves.

Swamp

The swamps of North Africa had shallow, muddy water. Suchomimus lived here, wading through the water hunting for fish.

Fern prairie

Vast plains were carpeted in ferns and moss. Plant eaters foraged here and were hunted, just like giraffes and zebras today.

How many types of dinosaur are there?

There are five main groups of dinosaurs, but countless creatures existed within them. These dinosaurs ruled our world for more than 165 million years.

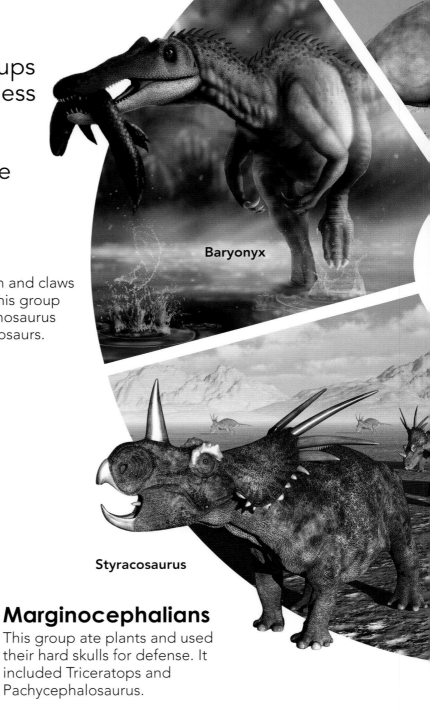

Baryonyx

Theropods

Theropods had sharp teeth and claws and walked on two legs. This group included the mighty Tyrannosaurus rex, as well as all flying dinosaurs.

Styracosaurus

? Picture quiz

What group does this dinosaur belong to?

See pages 130–131 for the answer.

Marginocephalians

This group ate plants and used their hard skulls for defense. It included Triceratops and Pachycephalosaurus.

Sauropodomorphs

These dinosaurs were the largest creatures to ever stomp across Earth. With their long necks and tails and massive bodies, they were the rulers of the dinosaur world.

Brachiosaurus

Ornithopods

Ornithopods were plant-eating dinosaurs notable for their strange head shapes. Some of their members had duckbill snouts (duck-like beaks).

Parasaurolophus

Family tree

By studying fossils, scientists can understand how the five main dinosaur groups were related to each other. The dinosaur family tree could look like this:

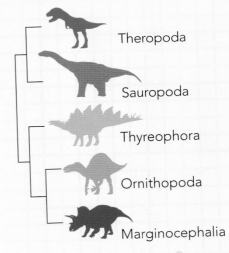

Theropoda

Sauropoda

Thyreophora

Ornithopoda

Marginocephalia

Ankylosaurus

Thyreophorans

Thyreophorans had thick, bony armor that protected their bodies. Many of them also had spiky tails.

Did dinosaurs live with sharks?

Sharks are ancient beasts. The first sharks, including Hybodus, lived alongside dinosaurs and existed for millions of years before them. Many of the animals we know now, however, appeared a long time after the dinosaurs became extinct.

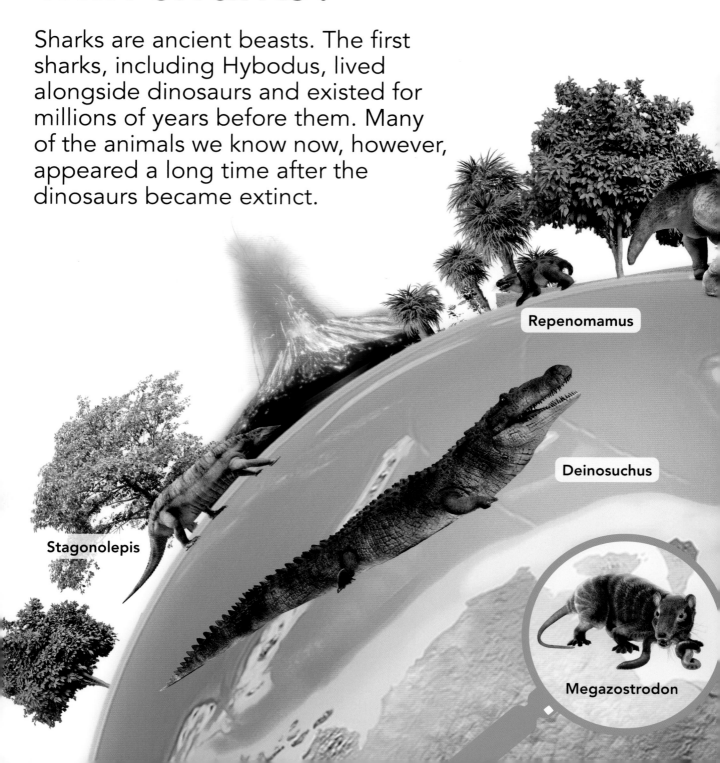

Repenomamus

Deinosuchus

Stagonolepis

Megazostrodon

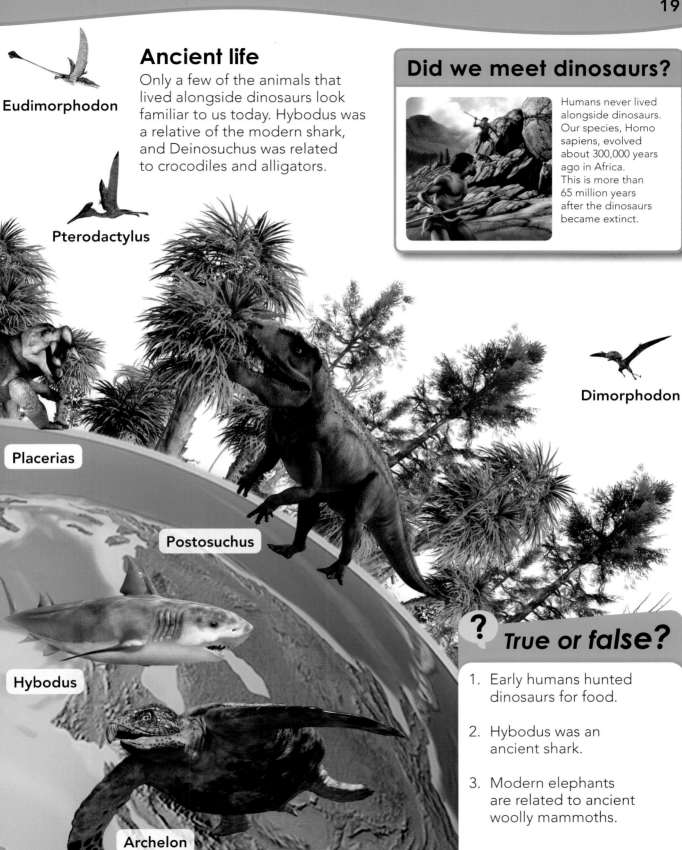

Ancient life

Only a few of the animals that lived alongside dinosaurs look familiar to us today. Hybodus was a relative of the modern shark, and Deinosuchus was related to crocodiles and alligators.

Eudimorphodon

Pterodactylus

Placerias

Postosuchus

Hybodus

Archelon

Dimorphodon

Did we meet dinosaurs?

Humans never lived alongside dinosaurs. Our species, Homo sapiens, evolved about 300,000 years ago in Africa. This is more than 65 million years after the dinosaurs became extinct.

? *True or false?*

1. Early humans hunted dinosaurs for food.

2. Hybodus was an ancient shark.

3. Modern elephants are related to ancient woolly mammoths.

See pages 130–131 for the answers.

Could humans survive in the dinosaur world?

Imagine sending a human family back in time to live in the Early Cretaceous period. Would they be able to survive? It would be very difficult. The world was a very different place then—with different animals, plants, and weather.

What plants could humans eat in the prehistoric world?

Ginkgo
Ginkgo trees are very ancient. Their berries are stinky but can be eaten. Unfortunately, most plants that we eat today evolved later than the Early Cretaceous.

Horsetail shoots
In the time of the dinosaurs, this common weed grew up to 100 ft (30 m) high. Humans can eat their mild-tasting shoots.

Pine nuts
Conifer trees have been around for about 300 million years. Their nuts would be a good source of fat and protein for human visitors.

Climate

In the Early Cretaceous, the weather was warmer than it is today. There was less oxygen and more carbon dioxide in the air. This would make it more difficult for humans to breathe.

? Quick quiz

1. What part of a conifer tree is good for humans to eat?

2. How long ago was the Cretaceous period?

3. How was the air different in the Cretaceous period?

See pages 130–131 for the answers.

Predators

This Deinonychus and other predators roamed the Cretaceous world. They probably hunted in packs, searching for a tasty meal—watch out, human time travelers!

Human intelligence

People use their intelligence to survive. Our family would soon build a shelter, make tools for hunting, and learn to find plants to eat. They would need to learn to make fire to cook food and scare away hungry predators.

What swam in the prehistoric sea?

Prehistoric oceans were home to sea monsters such as plesiosaurs, ichthyosaurs, and mosasaurs. These ancient beasts were not dinosaurs but marine reptiles. Mosasaurs are most closely related to modern lizards and snakes, while ichthyosaurs and plesiosaurs are more closely related to turtles.

What did they eat?

Ammonite

These ancient marine shellfish were a crunchy treat for any animal with strong enough jaws to break through their thick shells.

Each other

In the depths of the ocean, there's always a bigger sea monster. Smaller marine reptiles were eaten by the larger ones.

Ichthyosaurus

Icthyosaurus looked like a cross between a swordfish and a dolphin. It was a swift swimmer that ate squid and fish.

Elasmosaurus

This long-necked plesiosaur used its neck and needlelike teeth to snatch up fish.

Liopleurodon

This speedy plesiosaur had huge sharp teeth for grabbing fish and squid. It then swallowed them whole.

Mosasaurus

Everything was a meal to Mosasaurus. It could swallow sharks, diving seabirds, and other mosasaurs whole.

The massive Mosasaurus was 50 ft (15 m) long and weighed 5.5 tons (5 tonnes).

Albertonectes

This marine reptile had the longest neck of any known plesiosaur, with more than 76 vertebrae. Humans have seven.

? Quick quiz

1. What mythological creature was inspired by plesiosaurs?

2. How heavy was Mosasaurus?

3. How many neck vertebrae did Albertonectes have?

See pages 130–131 for the answers.

Which plants still grow today?

A lot has changed since dinosaurs were on Earth, but there are plants we see growing today that grew then, too! Some plants were only starting to appear back then. Grass grew for the first time just before dinosaurs became extinct.

Magnolia

Magnolias were some of the earliest plants to blossom in the world, first appearing during the Cretaceous period.

Cycads

These plants were all over Earth during the dinosaurs' time. Cycads are much less common today.

Ferns

Ferns provided the world with plenty of oxygen (the gas we need to breathe).

 The first ferns were around about 360 million years ago.

Monkey puzzle

Despite being covered in spiky leaves, this plant may have been eaten by long-necked sauropods.

What plants were growing?

Glossopteris leaf fossil
Known for its tongue-shaped leaves, this plant went extinct around 200 million years ago.

Alethopteris leaf fossil
Alethopteris was a plant that existed before the dinosaurs—roughly 360 to 300 million years ago.

Ginkgo

The earliest ginkgo grew around 270 million years ago. They are often called "living fossils" because they have remained almost the same since dinosaur times.

Moss

Much like today, moss covered the ground and trees in forests and swamps across the dinosaurs' world.

? Quick quiz

1. What type of leaf does a monkey puzzle have?

2. When did the first ferns exist on Earth?

3. What is the ginkgo plant sometimes known as?

See pages 130–131 for the answers.

Dinosaur anatomy

Scales, feathers, claws, clubs, horns, and frills—dinosaurs had many elaborate features. Some walked on two legs, while others stomped around on four. Some munched on tough plants with their flat chompers, while others shredded flesh to ribbons with their knifelike teeth.

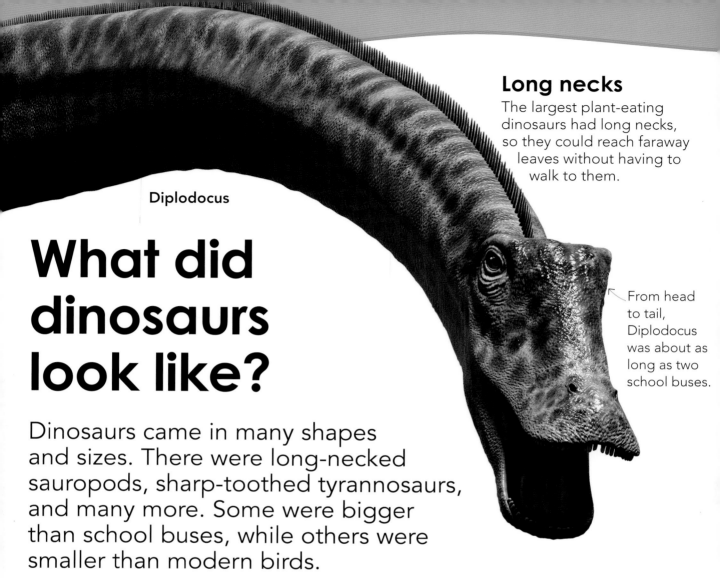

Long necks
The largest plant-eating dinosaurs had long necks, so they could reach faraway leaves without having to walk to them.

Diplodocus

What did dinosaurs look like?

Dinosaurs came in many shapes and sizes. There were long-necked sauropods, sharp-toothed tyrannosaurs, and many more. Some were bigger than school buses, while others were smaller than modern birds.

From head to tail, Diplodocus was about as long as two school buses.

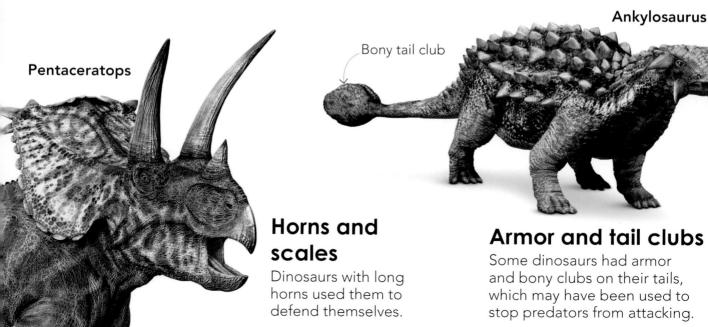

Ankylosaurus

Pentaceratops

Bony tail club

Horns and scales
Dinosaurs with long horns used them to defend themselves.

Armor and tail clubs
Some dinosaurs had armor and bony clubs on their tails, which may have been used to stop predators from attacking.

Did male and female Stegosaurus look different?

Female
New evidence shows that male and female Stegosaurus may have had different kinds of plates, with females having thinner ones than the males.

Male
Some scientists think that male Stegosaurus had bigger, rounder plates than females. The males may have used these large plates to attract mates.

Plates and spikes
Many dinosaurs defended themselves from predators and rivals with plates and spikes.

Kentrosaurus

Teeth
Meat-eating, or carnivorous, dinosaurs had mouths filled with sharp teeth. They were useful for tearing large chunks of flesh off their prey.

Allosaurus

Alxasaurus

Claws
Long claws may have helped dinosaurs dig for insects to eat, hold onto prey, or defend themselves from enemies.

? Quick quiz

1. How long was Diplodocus?

2. What did dinosaurs use their long claws for?

3. Did male Stegosauruses have bigger or smaller plates than females?

See pages 130–131 for the answers.

Did dinosaurs have feathers?

Yes, many dinosaurs were covered in them! These feathers grew on theropods, a group of dinosaurs that includes Tyrannosaurus rex and Velociraptor. Even though these dinosaurs had feathers like birds today do, many could not fly.

Archaeopteryx fossil

In 1860, one of the first feathered dinosaur fossils was found in Germany. Scientists named this fossil Archaeopteryx. This dinosaur was birdlike and lived on Earth around 150 million years ago.

Evidence of wings

This part of an Archaeopteryx fossil shows where a feather would have been on its wing.

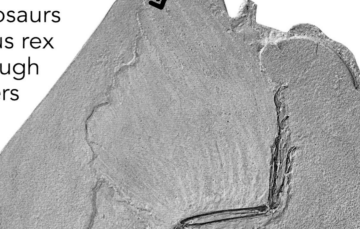

Archaeopteryx had a flat breastbone. It may not have had strong flight muscles or have been good at flying.

What types of feathers are there?

Bristles
Usually found around the necks and heads of some types of bird, bristles are thin, stiff feathers.

Fluffy feathers
These feathers keep birds warm and cover much of their bodies. This ostrich has lots of fluffy feathers all over its body.

Flying feathers
Some types of bird, such as owls, have flying feathers. They are smooth and designed to help birds fly quickly.

Wing claws
Early feathered dinosaurs had sharp claws on their wings. These are similar to the claws on bats' wings.

Short wings
Feathered dinosaurs had shorter wings than other flying creatures of the time, such as the pterosaurs.

Tail
Archaeopteryx's tail was long, bony, and covered with feathers.

Claws
With sharp claws, Archaeopteryx could grab and cut up tiny prey, such as lizards and insects.

? Quick quiz

1. When did Archaeopteryx live on Earth?

2. Why do some birds have fluffy feathers?

See pages 130–131 for the answers.

How big were dinosaurs?

Dinosaurs came in a wide range of sizes. The largest would tower over the tallest of today's animals, including giraffes and elephants. The smallest dinosaurs were the size of birds such as chickens.

? True or false?

1. The smallest dinosaurs were the size of humans.

2. Triceratops weighed more than an elephant.

3. The heaviest dinosaurs were plant eaters.

See pages 130–131 for the answers.

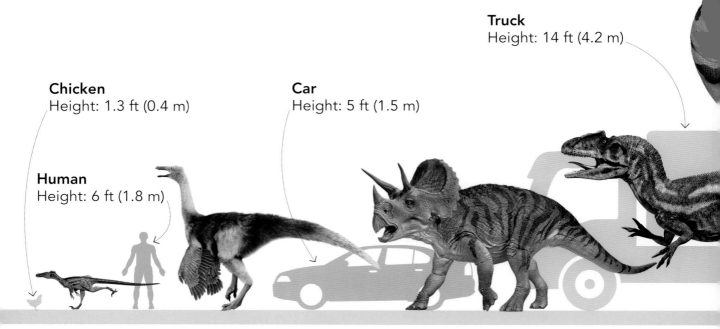

Truck
Height: 14 ft (4.2 m)

Chicken
Height: 1.3 ft (0.4 m)

Car
Height: 5 ft (1.5 m)

Human
Height: 6 ft (1.8 m)

Velociraptor
Length: 6.5 ft (2 m)
Height: 3 ft (0.9 m)
Unlike the ones in the movie *Jurassic World*, Velociraptors were not as big as humans.

Gallimimus
Length: 20 ft (6 m)
Hip height: 6.5 ft (2 m)
This ostrich-like dinosaur was more than twice the height of an adult human.

Triceratops
Length: 29.5 ft (9 m)
Height: 10 ft (3 m)
Triceratops was larger than a car and weighed up to 13 tons—far more than an elephant.

Which was the heaviest dinosaur?

Argentinosaurus

Weighing in at a mighty 66 to 99 tons, Argentinosaurus is believed to be the heaviest known dinosaur. It ate plants, and its fossils were found in Argentina, South America.

Three-story building
Height: 43 ft (13 m)

Allosaurus

Length: 29 ft (9 m)
Height: 13 ft (4 m)
These fearsome hunters were the top predator of their time and hunted dinosaurs like Stegosaurus and Diplodocus.

Dreadnoughtus

Length: 98.5 ft (30 m)
Shoulder height: 20 ft (6 m)
This giant was one of the longest dinosaurs. It lived 77 million years ago in the region that's now Patagonia, South America.

The name "Dreadnoughtus" means "fears nothing."

Did T. rex have a heart?

Only a mighty heart could power a killing machine like T. rex. Scientists think its heart had four chambers—like the hearts of birds and mammals. This type of heart would have been needed to pump blood around T. rex's enormous muscular body.

? Quick quiz

1. How many chambers do scientists think there were in T. rex's heart?

2. Did dinosaurs have red blood cells?

3. What was Camarasaurus's body temperature?

See pages 130–131 for the answers.

Heart sizes

T. rex had a very large heart—about 100 times heavier than a human heart. It was actually small for such a massive beast, but its four-chambered structure made it very effective at its job.

An African elephant's heart is rounder and much larger than a human heart. It weighs about 44 lb (20 kg).

A human heart is roughly the size of a large fist and weighs about 0.7 lb (300 g).

Crocodiles are the only living reptiles with four-chambered hearts.

Human heart

Crocodile heart

Elephant heart

Breathing

Animals breathe to get oxygen into their bodies. Dinosaurs such as T. rex had breathing systems similar to birds'. Birds' lungs receive oxygen from the air when they breathe in and when they breathe out, thanks to air sacs connected to the lungs. Mammals' lungs are different because they receive fresh oxygen only when they breathe in.

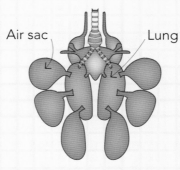

Breathing system in birds

Breathing system in mammals

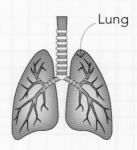

T. rex's huge heart weighed about 66 lb (30 kg).

T. rex heart

Were dinosaurs warm-blooded?

Camarasaurus

Scientists are still not sure whether dinosaurs were warm-blooded, cold-blooded, or a mixture of both. However, Camarasaurus was probably warm-blooded. By studying its teeth, researchers figured out that its body temperature was about 96.3°F (35.7°C).

Velociraptor

This theropod traveled around hunting, which suggests that it was warm-blooded. It also may have used its feathers to help control its body temperature.

How many bones did dinosaurs have?

It's hard to count how many bones a specific dinosaur species had because dinosaur skeletons are usually incomplete. The most complete T. rex skeleton ever discovered still contains only about 250 of the 380 bones it's thought to have had.

What shape were dinosaur hips?

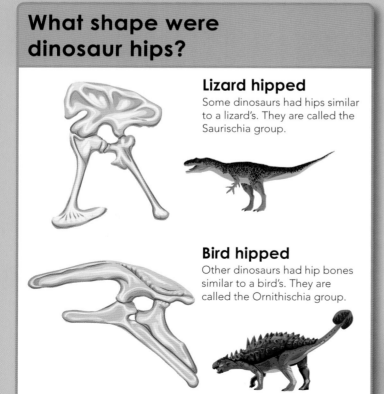

Lizard hipped
Some dinosaurs had hips similar to a lizard's. They are called the Saurischia group.

Bird hipped
Other dinosaurs had hip bones similar to a bird's. They are called the Ornithischia group.

Tail
T. rex had dozens of vertebrae in its long tail. It used its tail to help keep its heavy body balanced.

Joints
Joints are the places where two bones meet. Dinosaurs had a protective layer called cartilage over their joints, just as humans do, which let them move around smoothly.

The most complete T. rex skeleton ever discovered is known as "Sue."

Why weren't sauropods too heavy to stand?

Sauropods were immensely heavy. To support their huge bodies, they had very muscular legs, as thick as tree trunks. They also had long tails, which helped balance their massive weight, and their bones were surprisingly light.

Spinophorosaurus

Skull

A dinosaur's skull can show you what it ate. Sharp teeth usually mean it ate meat, while flat teeth mean it ate plants.

Gastralia

Some dinosaurs had bones called gastralia that were like a second set of ribs on their bellies. These may have helped with breathing.

? Quick quiz

1. What are gastralia?

2. Did all dinosaurs have sharp claws?

3. What two groups are dinosaurs divided into by their hip shapes?

See pages 130–131 for the answers.

What was the longest dinosaur?

The longest known dinosaurs were the titanosaurs, a type of sauropod. They had long tails and necks and massive bodies supported by pillar-like legs. The longest of all was Patagotitan.

Long neck

Patagotitan held its long neck almost horizontally. This let it stand in one place and sweep its neck from side to side to eat low-lying plants.

Patagotitan was longer than a blue whale but not as heavy.

Patagotitan

Patagotitan was 122 ft (37 m) from head to tail, making it the longest known dinosaur. The highest part of its body was about 23 ft (7 m).

Tallest dinosaurs

Sauroposeidon was the tallest dinosaur. It stood like a giraffe and belonged to a group of sauropods called brachiosaurids. Titanosaurs were longer, but they held their necks lower.

- Sauroposeidon
- Brachiosaurus
- Argentinosaurus
- Dreadnoughtus
- Patagotitan
- Human

132 ft (40 m)
99 ft (30 m)
66 ft (20 m)
33 ft (10 m)

66 ft (20 m)
33 ft (10 m)

How did dinosaurs get so big?

Sauropods ate huge amounts of plants, which were abundant and easy to find where they lived. Tons of leaves gave them the energy and nutrition they needed to grow into giants.

Large body

No modern animals except for whales come close to the size of giant sauropods.

Weight-bearing legs

Four large, muscular legs helped the giant sauropods, such as Patagotitan, carry their heavy bodies. These dinosaurs could weigh nearly 76 tons.

? Quick quiz

1. What was the longest dinosaur?

2. What modern animal is a similar size to giant sauropods?

3. What did sauropods eat?

See pages 130–131 for the answers.

How fast could dinosaurs run?

Ornithomimids are known as "bird mimics." Like modern-day ostriches, they had long necks, feathered bodies, and were fast on their feet. They were some of the speediest dinosaurs.

Struthiomimus

This quick and sleek ornithomimid lived 76–74 million years ago. It most likely ate plants, insects, and tiny animals.

Sharp claws

The claws on the legs of ornithomimids may have been useful for gripping the ground, as ostriches do. Clawed arms were useful for catching prey.

Could humans outrun dinosaurs?

Humans are distance champions, but in a sprint, we wouldn't stand a chance against most dinosaurs. There is some debate about whether a human could outrun a T. rex... but you probably wouldn't have been able to try!

? Picture quiz

Which modern-day animal (pictured) has been compared to ornithomimids?

See pages 130–131 for the answer.

Tail

Their long, feathered tails helped balance out ornithomimids' bodies, helping them run quickly.

Powerful legs

Ornithomimids' strong leg muscles helped them reach speeds of up to 50 mph (80 kph).

Did dinosaurs have armor?

Some dinosaurs, including ankylosaurs, had bony plates and ridges covering their bodies like armor to defend themselves. They also had spikes and tail clubs, which acted as weapons for fighting back.

Mighty club
The tail club was a powerful weapon that could be used for defense and attack. It was heavy enough to kill some of Ankylosaurus's predators.

Bony back
Ankylosaurus's back was covered with rows of oval bony plates. Some of this armor included large, horned spikes.

Bone crusher

Dinosaurs such as T. rex had thick, heavy skulls and sharp, serrated teeth for biting down on prey and challengers with brute force.

How else did ankylosaurs protect themselves?

Eyelids

Ankylosaurs were covered with bony plates. They even had plates on their eyelids, which protected their eyes.

Shoulder spikes

Their shoulders were covered in spikes, which ankylosaurs used as weapons to protect themselves against enemies.

Helmet head

Ankylosaurus's head was like a very tough helmet. It was covered with interlocking bony plates that may have been attached to its skull.

What were horns for?

Triceratops used its three fearsome horns to attract mates and protect itself from predators and rivals. Larger horns drew more attention from potential partners and provided better defense against enemies.

Keratin

Triceratops horns were made of bone covered in keratin—a material also found in bird beaks and your fingernails.

In battle

Triceratops may have locked horns like this during a fight with each other.

? Quick quiz

1. Where do we find keratin?

2. How big did a Triceratops frill grow?

3. Name three modern-day animals that lock horns.

See pages 130–131 for the answers.

Which modern-day animals lock horns?

Impalas

Impalas roam African savannas (grassy plains). These small antelopes use their horns to defend against predators such as hyenas and cheetahs, as well as to battle with each other.

Deer

Male deer use their antlers to fight with other males, especially during the breeding season. They will bend down and fight with their spiky headgear.

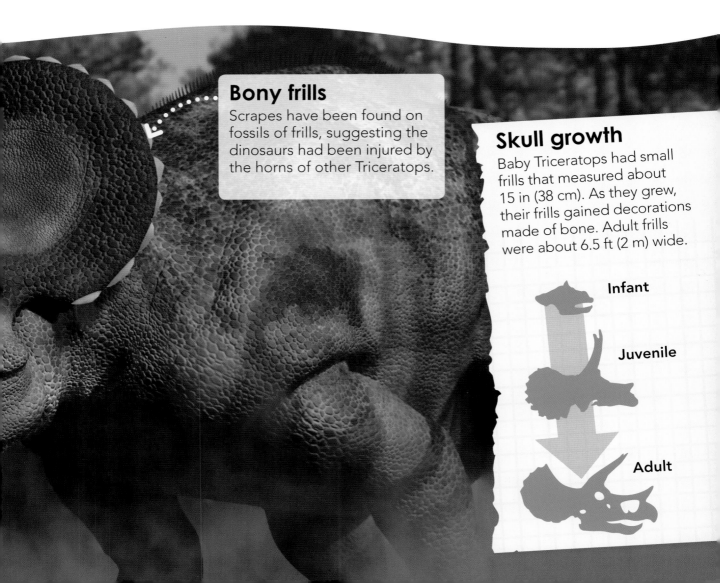

Bony frills

Scrapes have been found on fossils of frills, suggesting the dinosaurs had been injured by the horns of other Triceratops.

Skull growth

Baby Triceratops had small frills that measured about 15 in (38 cm). As they grew, their frills gained decorations made of bone. Adult frills were about 6.5 ft (2 m) wide.

Infant

Juvenile

Adult

How small was the smallest dinosaur?

The smallest dinosaur ever could have fit in the palm of your hand and was roughly the size of a sparrow. This tiny dromaeosaur was related to Velociraptor.

Dinosaur tracks

In 2018, scientists discovered 110-million-year-old footprints on a piece of rock in South Korea. The tiny tracks, which measured only 0.4 in (1 cm) long, were the smallest dinosaur footprints ever found. The creature has not yet been named, but its tracks are called Dromaeosauriformipes rarus.

? Quick quiz

1. When did scientists discover the fossil of Anchiornis huxleyi?

2. Which dinosaur was the same size as a pigeon?

3. What are the smallest dinosaur tracks ever found called?

See pages 130–131 for the answers.

Have fossils been found of small dinosaurs?

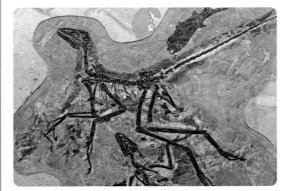

In 2009, scientists found the fossil of Anchiornis huxleyi, which was as small as a chicken. This dinosaur lived between roughly 150 and 160 million years ago. It may have used its feathers to parachute from tree branch to tree branch.

Some microraptors had four wings—two on their arms and two on their legs.

Other small dinosaurs

There were many tiny dinosaurs that lived on Earth millions of years ago. Most of them were covered in feathers, such as the pigeon-sized Epidexipteryx, and may have looked a bit like little birds.

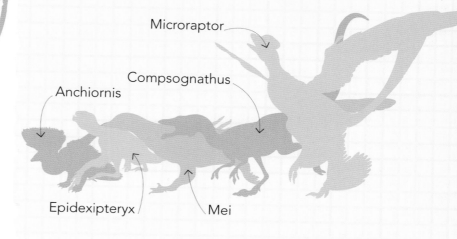

Microraptor

Compsognathus

Anchiornis

Epidexipteryx

Mei

What did dinosaurs eat?

Many dinosaurs were herbivores, which means that they ate plants. Others, however, were carnivores who ate meat—even the meat of dead dinosaurs! There were also omnivores, who ate both meat and plants.

Scientists can study dinosaurs' fossilized poop, called coprolites, to see what they ate.

Spinosaurus

Carnivores
Pointy teeth and sharp claws were the tools of meat-eating dinosaurs. These helped carnivores, such as Spinosaurus and Velociraptor, catch and kill their prey.

Herbivores
Plant-eating dinosaurs, such as the sauropods, needed to support their large bodies. They did this by constantly eating lots of ferns and leaves.

How did dinosaurs digest their food?

Plant eaters may have swallowed smooth stones called gastroliths to help them digest food. Once in the stomach, the gastroliths would have been able to grind up plants dinosaurs had eaten.

Gastroliths

? Quick quiz

1. Which dinosaurs ate the widest variety of foods?

2. What type of food did herbivores eat?

3. What would Triceratops have eaten?

See pages 130–131 for the answers.

Argentinosaurus

Therizinosaurus

Omnivores

Omnivores ate whatever they could find. These dinosaurs might dine on plants and berries one day, and insects and lizards the next.

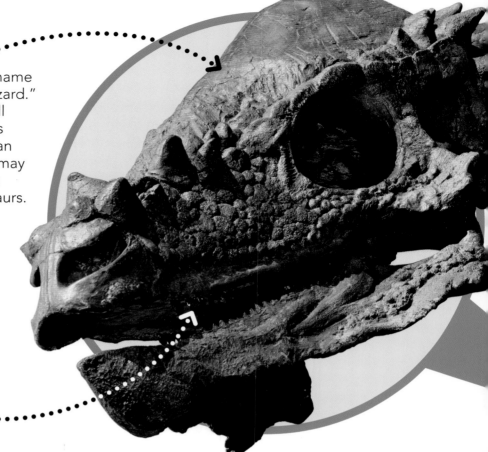

Bony dome

Pachycephalosaurus's name means "thickheaded lizard." At 10 in (25 cm), its skull was more than 40 times the thickness of a human skull! This bony dome may have been used during fights with other dinosaurs.

Specialized teeth

Pachycephalosaurus probably feasted mostly on plants, chewing them with its leaf-shaped teeth. However, it also had pointy front teeth, like those of a meat-eating dinosaur.

Why did Pachycephalosaurus have such a bony head?

Scientists have butted heads over why Pachycephalosaurus had such a bony dome. Some think it used its skull to ram into rivals, but more recently, they believe it was used to draw attention from mates.

Spiky crowns

Spiky bones surrounded the roof of this thickheaded dinosaur's skull. The crown may have helped make the dinosaur look more attractive to potential mates.

Scaly skin

Pachycephalosaurus's body was probably covered in scaly skin, which protected it from insect bites and thorns.

Which other dinosaurs had bony heads?

Acrotholus

This bony-headed dinosaur was much smaller than Pachycephalosaurus. Its skull was about 2 in (3 cm) thick.

Stygimoloch

Some paleontologists think that specimens found of Stygimoloch could actually just belong to young Pachycephalosaurus.

Beaked mouth

With its short beak, the front of its face resembled that of a bird. The beak helped the dinosaur eat plants.

? Quick quiz

1. How thick was a Pachycephalosaurus skull?

2. What did Pachycephalosaurus use its spiky head for?

3. What did Pachycephalosaurus eat?

See pages 130–131 for the answers.

Small, muscular arms

Despite their small size, T. rex's arms may have been powerful. Some scientists estimate they could carry roughly 440 lb (200 kg).

Why did T. rex have such short arms?

Scientists don't know exactly what T. rex's tiny arms were for. This mighty dinosaur may have used its short arms for catching and holding down prey, or to lift its bulky body off the ground.

Vicious claws

The two sharp claws on T. rex's arms could measure more than 6 in (15 cm) long.

Huge body

T. rex was more than 40 ft (12 m) long and may have weighed more than a small truck!

Did all tyrannosauroids have short arms?

Guanlong wucaii

This tyrannosauroid lived 160 million years ago. It had larger arms than T. rex which it may have used to catch prey. It was much smaller than a T. rex at only 3 ft (1.1 m) tall.

Moros intrepidus

Moros intrepidus was a tyrannosauroid that lived 96 million years ago. It was the size of a deer, but we do not know how big its arms were.

Large feet

T. rex walked around on two thick, birdlike feet. Each foot had three large toes with sharp claws.

? Quick quiz

1. How much weight could T. rex's arms hold?
   a) 440 lb (200 kg)
   b) 880 lb (400 kg)
   c) 1,320 lb (600 kg)

2. Was T. rex an herbivore or a carnivore?

See pages 130–131 for the answers.

How big were T. rex's teeth?

No creature had a scarier smile than T. rex. Its mouth was filled with 60 dagger-like teeth, which were between around 9 in (23 cm) and 12 in (31 cm) long.

Size comparison

A single T. rex tooth was about the size of an entire velociraptor skull, and it was almost double the length of a banana!

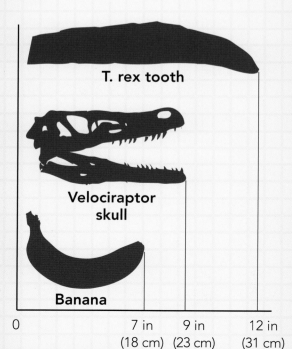

T. rex tooth

Velociraptor skull

Banana

| 0 | 7 in (18 cm) | 9 in (23 cm) | 12 in (31 cm) |

Serrated teeth

Each tooth had tiny serrated (sawlike) edges, which helped T. rex tear skin and flesh from the bones of its prey.

Giant jaws

T. rex could crush animal bones with its huge, powerful jaws.

Light skull

Holes between bones, called fenestrae, made T. rex's massive skull lighter.

Some scientists think that T. rex may have had the strongest bite of any animal!

Was T. rex a hunter or a scavenger?

Scientists disagree about whether T. rex was a hunter who stalked and killed its prey, or a scavenger who ate dead animals. It's possible that T. rex was a predator who both hunted and scavenged.

? Quick quiz

1. How many teeth did T. rex have?

2. What other dinosaur's skull was around the same size as a T. rex tooth?

3. Did fenestrae make T. rex's skull lighter or heavier?

See pages 130–131 for the answers.

Did all dinosaurs have tails?

Yes, all dinosaurs had tails. Some doubled as weapons, with fearsome spikes or a thick club at the end. Other dinosaurs used their tails for balance, camouflage, or to help them move more swiftly while hunting.

Massive sauropods, such as Diplodocus and Supersaurus, had the longest tails.

Clubbed tail

Euoplocephalus could swing its clubbed tail like a war hammer, and its body had thick armor covered in spikes. This dinosaur was a tough opponent for any predator.

Euoplocephalus

A powerful swing of this club could crack bone.

Long, thin tail

Some dinosaurs with very long necks, such as Diplodocus, had tails that were just as long.

Diplodocus

Spiked tail

Stegosaurus had a spiked tail that made predators think twice about risking a fight. Some spikes were more than 3.3 ft (1 m) long.

Stegosaur

Caudipteryx

Feathered tail

Many small theropods, such as Caudipteryx, had feathered tails. We don't know if these were used for flight, but they might have given rise to the feathered tails seen in today's birds.

Have any fossilized tails been found?

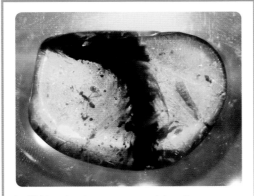

In 2016, scientists announced the discovery of a feathered dinosaur tail. It was encased in amber, which is a fossilized sticky substance made by trees. The tail probably belonged to a small, sparrow-sized coelurosaur.

Striped tail

Well-preserved remains of Sinosauropteryx show that its tail feathers probably had brown and white stripes, which provided camouflage.

Sinosauropteryx

Spiked club tail

Some dinosaurs, such as Shunosaurus, had clubbed tails armed with small spikes. It most likely used its tail to defend itself from predators.

Shunosaurus

The overall length of an adult Shunosaurus was about 31 ft (9.5 m).

Albertosaurus

Balancing tail

Albertosaurus had a huge tail that balanced the weight of its large head and body. Many large dinosaurs needed a heavy tail to be able to balance when standing and also to move swiftly.

? Quick quiz

1. Which dinosaurs had the longest tails?

2. Did dinosaurs have bones in their tails?

3. Which dinosaur had a striped tail?

See pages 130–131 for the answers.

How big were dinosaur eggs?

Every dinosaur, from the mighty titanosaurs to the tiny microraptors, laid eggs, just as chickens do today. By studying fossilized dinosaur eggs, scientists have learned about their size and, in some cases, even their color.

Apatosaurus egg

Apatosaurus eggs were larger than basketballs. A fully grown Apatosaurus was a huge plant-eating dinosaur.

Tarbosaurus egg

Tarbosaurus was a cousin of T. rex. Its eggs have been found in Mongolia and China.

Oviraptor egg

Scientists at first mistook these eggs for Protoceratops eggs and thought Oviraptors were egg thieves.

Tennis ball 2.5 in (6.5 cm) long

Did dinosaurs have nests?

Open nest
Some dinosaurs laid their eggs in large, open nests. Many theropods, which are closely related to birds, used this tactic.

Buried clutches
Most dinosaurs buried their eggs beneath heaps of sand to protect them from hungry predators.

? True or false?

1. Tarbosaurus eggs have been found in Japan and Australia.

2. Most dinosaurs laid their eggs in large, open batches.

3. An Apatosaurus egg was larger than a basketball.

See pages 130–131 for the answers.

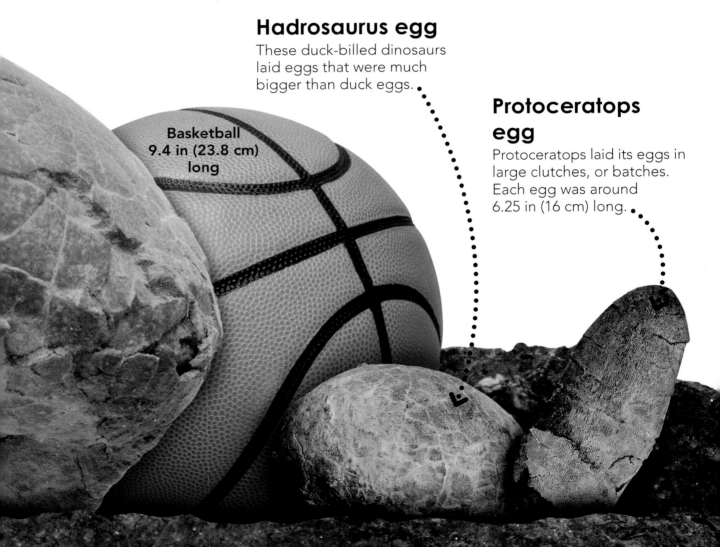

Hadrosaurus egg
These duck-billed dinosaurs laid eggs that were much bigger than duck eggs.

Basketball 9.4 in (23.8 cm) long

Protoceratops egg
Protoceratops laid its eggs in large clutches, or batches. Each egg was around 6.25 in (16 cm) long.

What was the weirdest-looking dinosaur?

With its unique mixture of scythe-like claws, gangly neck, and large potbelly, Therizinosaurus is among the most bizarre dinosaurs discovered so far. It was a therapod, related to the Velociraptor, but ate mostly plants and lived 75 million years ago.

Long neck

At about 10 ft (3 m) long, Therizinosaurus's neck was longer than a giraffe's. It had a long tail too, and its total body length was 33 ft (10 m).

Giraffe

? Quick quiz

1. How long were Therizinosaurus's claws?
   a) 4 in (10 cm)
   b) 12 in (30 cm)
   c) 3.3 ft (1 m)

2. What dinosaur had stubby, one-clawed arms?
   a) Therizinosaurus
   b) Kosmoceratops
   c) Linhenykus

See pages 130–131 for the answers.

Claw fossil

Long claws

Therizinosaurus's curved claws were 3.3 ft (1 m) long. They were probably used to drag plants into its mouth.

Potbelly

Like a leaf-eating monkey, Therizinosaurus had a potbelly, or round stomach, where vegetation was slowly digested, or broken down.

Proboscis monkey

What other dinosaurs had strange features?

Linhenykus

This dinosaur looked like a miniature ostrich but with stubby, one-clawed arms. It may have used its claws to dig into termite nests.

Epidexipteryx

This tiny dinosaur had long, strange-looking tail feathers. They didn't help it fly but were probably used to create dazzling displays to attract a mate.

Kosmoceratops

Many-horned Kosmoceratops had a very interesting head. Eight horns curled downward, while two stuck out above its eyebrows.

Senses and behavior

In the dangerous Mesozoic world, dinosaurs needed all five senses to survive. A keen sense of smell led T. rex to its prey, while Yi qi used its strong sight to spot any danger.

What did dinosaurs do all day?

The daily goal for dinosaurs was survival. They needed to make sure that they lived long enough to see the next day. To do this, dinosaurs spent their time finding food, escaping predators, protecting their homes, and taking care of their young.

Carnotaurus

? Quick quiz

1. What are the round bones found in a dinosaur's eye called?

2. Was Carnotaurus a carnivore or an herbivore?

3. What food did Diplodocus eat?

See pages 130–131 for the answers.

Looking after their territory

Some dinosaurs, such as Carnotaurus, may have been very protective of their territory. They would battle enemies to make sure that their homes were not taken from them.

Looking for food

For some dinosaurs, such as the plant-eating Diplodocus, finding food was as easy as finding plants with tasty leaves. For others, however, every meal was a struggle, and they had to spend a long time looking for the right food.

Diplodocus

Maiasaura

Could dinosaurs see at night?

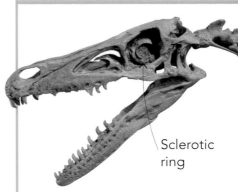

Sclerotic ring

Many dinosaurs had sets of round bones in their eyes to help hold them in place. By studying this set of bones, known as the sclerotic ring, some scientists think that these dinosaurs could see at night. However, others don't believe this is enough proof.

Looking after the young

Fossils show that some dinosaurs, such as Maiasaura, spent time looking after their children. Dinosaur parents probably spent most of their day feeding their young and protecting them from predators.

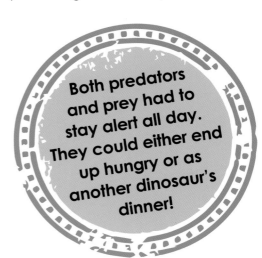

Both predators and prey had to stay alert all day. They could either end up hungry or as another dinosaur's dinner!

⌐·····.Throat

Scientists think that dinosaur throats were similar to those of birds and crocodiles.

Making sounds

Scientists have used crocodile and bird noises to re-create the sound they think dinosaurs made. Dinosaurs probably created a deep, grumbling sound rather than a roar, which would have been felt as well as heard.

Did dinosaurs roar?

That fearsome T. rex roar you've heard on screen may just be movie magic, because scientists think it might not have roared at all. Instead, it probably let out a rumbling boom that would still have sent shivers down your spine.

? Quick quiz

1. Did T. rex's mouth need to be open to make a noise?

2. What vibrates inside our throats to make sounds?

3. What animal sounds can be mixed together to make dinosaur noises in movies?

See pages 130–131 for the answers.

How birds sing

We have a larynx, or voice box, at the top of our windpipe. It contains vocal cords that vibrate to make sounds. Modern birds have a syrinx, with two branches, at the bottom of their windpipe instead. Both branches vibrate separately so birds can make two sounds at the same time.

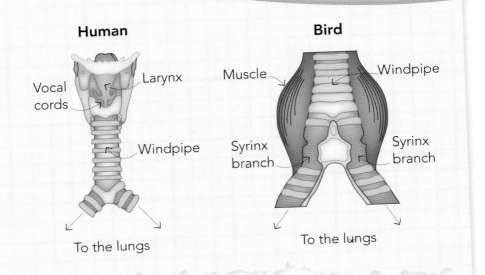

Human

Vocal cords

Larynx

Windpipe

To the lungs

Bird

Muscle

Windpipe

Syrinx branch

Syrinx branch

To the lungs

Jaws

T. rex had massive jaws, but it didn't need to open them to make a noise. Scientists think that T. rex could have made a noise with its mouth shut, as reptiles and birds do.

Did baby dinosaurs play?

Yes, probably! One way scientists learn about dinosaurs is by looking at how animals related to them behave. Young birds, crocodiles, and alligators have been seen playing and seeming to have fun. So, baby dinosaurs could well have done the same.

Were dinosaurs good parents?

Scientists think some dinosaurs, such as Oviraptors, were thoughtful parents that spent large amounts of time watching over and caring for their nests.

Maiasaura stayed close to their mothers even after they left the nest. They lived in big herds of hundreds.

Maiasaura

Some dinosaurs, like Maiasaura, were raised in nests near each other and were cared for by their parents while young. This means they may have had opportunities to play and interact with each other.

Playful

Baby dinosaurs may have played with each other or with objects. Similar behaviors have been seen in baby crocodiles and birds.

Babies

When a baby Maiasaura hatched, it was only about 12 in (30 cm) long, which is about the size of this book! However, they grew to be massive—up to 30 ft (9 m) long.

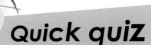

Safety

Young dinosaurs that lived in herds may have found safety from predators by staying close to their parents or other large members of their group, as baby elephants and wildebeests do today.

? Quick quiz

1. What modern-day animals do scientists study to learn about dinosaur behavior?

2. What dinosaur was mislabeled an "egg thief"?

3. How large could herds of Maiasaura get?

See pages 130–131 for the answers.

What were frills, sails, and crests for?

Dinosaurs loved to show off. Many had fancy frills on their faces, colorful crests on their heads, or stunning sails on their backs. These features probably helped attract potential mates.

Citipati

This birdlike dinosaur had a crest of bone and keratin on its head. Keratin is what human hair and nails are made of.

Some curved head crests could make a loud trumpet sound.

Neck frills helped dinosaurs show how attractive they were.

Pentaceratops

At 7.5 ft (2.3 m) tall, the colossal neck frills on Pentaceratops gave this three-horned dinosaur the largest skull of any land animal.

Corythosaurus

This dinosaur was so named because its head crest looks like the helmet of an ancient Corinthian soldier.

Cryolophosaurus

This carnivorous dinosaur had a crest on top of its head that looked like a fan or a tiny crown.

What do modern-day animals have to show off with?

Elephant seal
Male elephant seals have floppy, dangling noses they use to attract females. They also use their noses to make loud roars.

Peacock
Male peacocks shake their beautiful blue-and-green tail feathers to show female peahens how attractive they are.

The longest known dinosaur crest belonged to Parasaurolophus. It was 3.3 ft (1 m) long.

Nose crests may have been used to make mating calls.

Muttaburrasaurus
Muttaburrasaurus had a bulging lump on its muzzle. It may have used this bulbous nose to make loud noises for communicating.

Sails could have been used to control body temperature.

Ouranosaurus
Ouranosaurus had a large sail on its back that was supported by spines connected to its backbone.

? Quick quiz

1. Which dinosaur had a crown-like crest on the top of its head?

2. Do female peahens have colorful tail feathers?

See pages 130–131 for the answers.

Who was more powerful, T. rex or Spinosaurus?

These two meat eaters were titans of the dinosaur world. Both had muscular, agile bodies and many dagger-like teeth. Spinosaurus was larger with strong arms, but T. rex could destroy flesh and bone between its mighty jaws. However, they would never have actually faced off because they lived at different times and on opposite ends of the world.

T. rex

The bone-crushing bite of this 11-ton monster made it the most fearsome dinosaur ever to prowl across prehistoric North America and Asia.

Teeth

T. rex's mouth was lined with more than 60 sharp teeth. Some were as big as bananas, with jagged edges like a steak knife.

? Quick quiz

1. Which dinosaur had the most powerful bite?

2. What was the unusual feature on Spinosaurus's back?

3. Would Spinosaurus and T. rex have met in the wild?

See pages 130–131 for the answers.

Sail spines

Spinosaurus had a "sail" on its back that was made up of several spines, up to 7 ft (2 m) long, connected by skin. It made the dinosaur look bigger and scarier to any would-be attacker.

Spinosaurus

Spinosaurus lived in North Africa, and its sharp teeth chomped up fish—it would have given any attacker a nasty bite!

Spinosaurus is the largest known meat-eating dinosaur.

Could dinosaurs swim?

It's possible that not all dinosaurs were strictly land dwellers. There is evidence that some dinosaurs, such as Suchomimus, may have been able to swim too. Suchomimus would have snatched fish in the shallow water.

Did other dinosaurs go in the water?

Spinosaurus
The giant predator Spinosaurus might have been able to swim. Spinosaurus's needlelike teeth were probably used for trapping and spearing fish.

Crocodile like

Suchomimus means "crocodile mimic." Its long skull and narrow jaws were similar to those of a crocodile.

Fishing

Suchomimus's long jaws held more than 120 sharp teeth, which were perfectly suited to catching fish.

? Quick quiz

1. What were Spinosaurus's needlelike teeth used for?

2. Was Suchomimus a carnivore?

3. Which living reptile has a skull similar to that of Suchomimus?

See pages 130–131 for the answers.

Did dinosaurs have friends?

Some dinosaurs spent a lot of time hanging out together. For plant-eating dinosaurs, living with other dinosaurs helped stop predators from attacking them, while meat eaters hunted in packs to take down bigger prey.

Dinosaurs didn't just hang out together—they also ate, slept, and traveled in herds.

Herd of Uberabatitan

Protecting the young
Some dinosaurs fiercely protected their children. A few prehistoric parents have been found fossilized with their young nestled around them.

What other animals live in groups?

Zebras

Living and traveling in a herd gives zebras protection from their many predators. They are hunted by animals who can lurk unseen in the tall grasses of the African savanna.

Lions

Lions live and hunt in groups, known as prides. This lets them work together to kill large animals, such as zebras and wildebeests, for food.

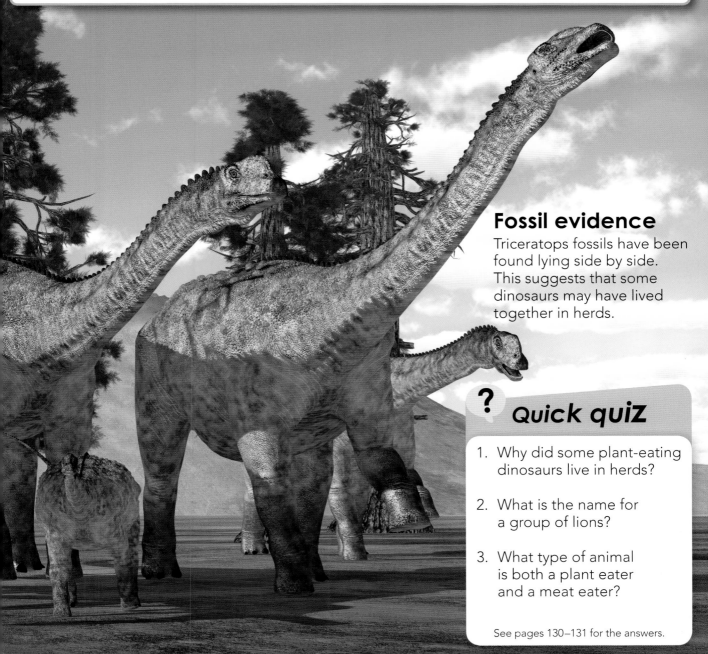

Fossil evidence

Triceratops fossils have been found lying side by side. This suggests that some dinosaurs may have lived together in herds.

? Quick quiz

1. Why did some plant-eating dinosaurs live in herds?

2. What is the name for a group of lions?

3. What type of animal is both a plant eater and a meat eater?

See pages 130–131 for the answers.

Wings

Pterosaur wings were made of thin, leathery skin attached to the limbs and sides of the body.

Walking on all fours

Fossil tracks made by prehistoric flying reptiles suggest that they walked on all fours when on land. They folded their wings and used their fingers to support the front part of their body.

Wings stretched out for flapping

Wings folded for walking

In the air

On land

Feet

Pterosaurs had small feet. These helped keep the reptiles streamlined during flight, so they could sail easily through the air.

Were pterosaurs dinosaurs?

No! It's a common mistake, but pterosaurs were not dinosaurs. While some dinosaurs may have been able to fly and glide, it was pterosaurs that seized the skies. Pterosaurs were flying reptiles. They included Pterodactylus and Pteranodon.

Crest

Many pterosaurs had colorful head crests. Some were wide and fan-shaped, while others were thin and pointy, like a dagger.

How big were pterosaurs?

Quetzalcoatlus

Pterosaurs were the largest animals ever to fly. The colossal Quetzalcoatlus had a wingspan of 33 ft (10 m), which is similar to that of a fighter jet.

Beak

This pterosaur, called Tupandactylus imperator, had a toothless beak with a small crest under the lower jaw.

Fingers

Pterosaurs had three clawed fingers close together and a fourth, super-long finger that stretched to the wing's end.

Pterosaurs had lightweight hollow bones with thin walls. This made flying easier.

? Quick quiz

1. How did pterosaurs' bones make flying easier?

2. Did pterosaurs flap their wings or simply glide?

3. How big were the smallest pterosaurs?

See pages 130–131 for the answers.

Did dinosaurs eat each other?

Some dinosaurs, such as Tyrannosaurus rex, hunted other dinosaurs for food. These meat-eating, or carnivorous, dinosaurs had to be strong to catch and devour their prey.

T. rex's bite was about four times as strong as an alligator's.

Strong jaws
T. rex had powerful jaws that helped it crush its prey.

T. rex and Triceratops

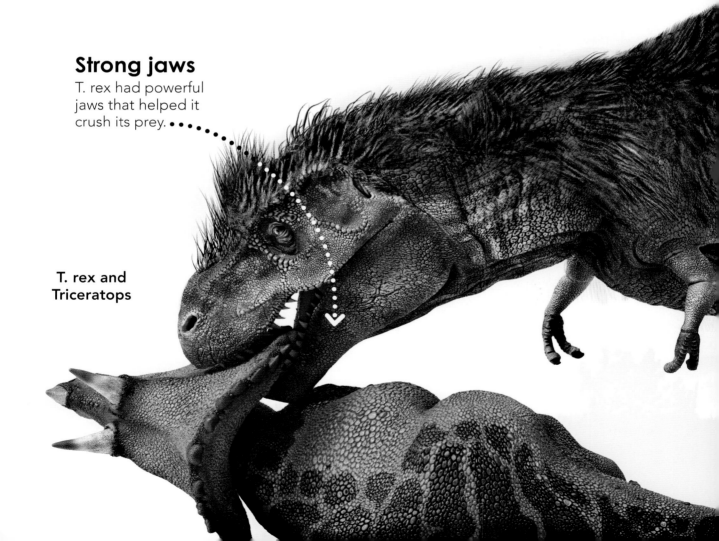

Jaw size

By examining dinosaur skull fossils, scientists have found that a dinosaur's jaw gape (the widest it could open its mouth) varied depending on its diet.

Allosaurus skull

Erlikosaurus skull

Carnivores

Meat-eating dinosaurs like Allosaurus would have had to grab on to animals using their jaws. Their jaw gapes were large and wide, allowing them to grab and bite flesh more easily.

Herbivores

Herbivores, such as Erlikosaurus, ate plants, leaves, and other vegetation. They did not need a lot of bite force and had smaller jaw gapes compared to carnivores.

Balancing tail

T. rex had a long tail that helped it balance its massive head, which was important when it was chasing down prey.

Walking speed

T. rex may have been able to reach top speeds of 11–25 mph (17–40 kph).

? Quick quiz

1. What is the difference between the jaws of carnivorous and herbivorous dinosaurs?

2. How fast could a T. rex run?

See pages 130–131 for the answers.

Vision
Stegosaurus probably had poor eyesight due to how small its brain and eyes were.

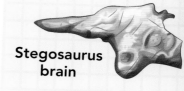

Stegosaurus brain

Banana

Brain size
This is where Stegosaurus's brain sat in its skull.

How big was Stegosaurus's brain?

Stegosaurus was as big as a minivan but had a brain that was about the same size as a dog's. This was minuscule for a dinosaur of its size. However, Stegosaurus was not stupid! It was a very successful dinosaur.

Small head
Like many large grazing dinosaurs, Stegosaurus had a small head.

Banana brain

Stegosaurus's brain was a similar shape to a banana.

? Picture quiz

Which dinosaur (pictured) had a small body but relatively large brain?

See pages 130–131 for the answer.

How big are animals' brains?

Ostrich
Ostriches have tiny brains that weigh about 1 oz (26 g). This is smaller than one of their eyeballs!

Elephant
An African elephant brain weighs about 12 lb (5.5 kg). This makes it about three times bigger than a human brain.

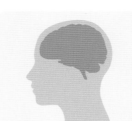

Human
Humans have large brains compared to our body sizes. Our brains weigh about 3.5 lb (1.5 kg).

Did dinosaurs use camouflage?

The dinosaur world was full of danger. Small creatures had to find ways to stay alive. They ran, hid, and even used camouflage to blend in with their surroundings to escape predators. By studying fossils, scientists have found that a dinosaur called Sinosauropteryx used a type of camouflage called countershading.

Herd of impala

Dark back

Sinosauropteryx had dark feathers covering the upper side of its body.

Striped tail

This dinosaur had a stripy orange-brown and white tail. This tail may have been used as camouflage to hide from predators.

Sinosauropteryx

Light underbelly

Sinosauropteryx had white feathers on its belly, which made it harder for predators to spot in sunlight.

Countershading

The sun lights the top half of an animal's body and casts a shadow on its underside. Animals that display countershading are darker on top and lighter underneath. This balances out the shadows cast by the sun, making the dinosaur look one flat color, which helps disguise it against its environment.

Normal shadows

Countershading

Hard to see dinosaur

? Quick quiz?

1. What is countershading?

2. What color were the feathers on the body of Anchiornis?

3. Which dinosaur used countershading to camouflage itself?

See pages 130–131 for the answers.

Impala

Modern animals such as impala also display countershading. Their darker upper body and lighter underside make them appear camouflaged.

Do we know what color other dinosaurs were?

Anchiornis

Scientists discovered colors in fossils of Anchiornis, a four-winged dinosaur. After studying these fossils, some scientists think that Anchiornis had red feathers around its head, and gray, black, and white feathers on its body.

Could dinosaurs climb trees?

Scientists think that some small feathered dinosaurs climbed trees. Clinging to branches and treetops was useful for early gliding dinosaurs, such as Yi qi. From high up, they could launch themselves across the forest in search of prey or away from danger.

Yi qi

This crow-sized dinosaur lived about 160 million years ago. It glided between trees, using its leathery wings. The only fossil of Yi qi was found in China.

Feathered body

Yi qi's body was covered in brushlike feathers, which were different from the long, sleek feathers on most birds. However, climbing dinosaurs did have long tail feathers.

What other animals can glide?

Flying squirrel
Flying squirrels use loose flaps of skin between their arms and legs as parachutes to glide between trees. Small movements of their legs let them steer.

Flying dragon
These little lizards have extra-long ribs with folds of skin between them. The lizards extend these ribs to glide between trees in their forest home.

Quick quiz

1. How big was the climbing dinosaur Yi qi?

2. What modern-day animals glide like Yi qi?

3. Where was the only fossil of Yi qi found?

See pages 130–131 for the answers.

Leathery wings

Unlike many other early flyers, Yi qi had leathery wings, which means it may have flown more like a bat than a bird. The wings also had sharp claws.

Clawed feet

Yi qi had four long toes with sharp claws, which probably helped it climb trees like a squirrel. The long toes may also have been used to push off into the air to glide.

How do modern animals sleep?

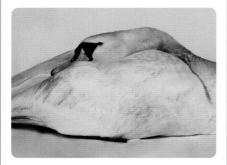

Swan

A swan folds back its neck and tucks its head under a wing to sleep. They can sleep floating on water or standing on one leg.

Australian bearded dragon

Scientists have found that Australian bearded dragons can experience the same deep sleep as humans.

Mei long means "soundly sleeping dragon" in Chinese.

Warm feathers

The feathers on some dinosaurs may have helped keep them warm at night. These feathers acted as a kind of blanket.

Did dinosaurs sleep?

Yes, dinosaurs went to sleep, just like you do. Some dinosaurs, such as the duck-sized Mei long, curled up into balls with their legs tucked in, as birds do when they sleep.

Sleeping dinosaur

In 2004, scientists discovered a fossil of a small dinosaur that was in a position similar to that of modern birds when they sleep. They named it Mei long.

Mei long

This slumbering dinosaur may have died during a volcanic eruption. It was buried in a blanket of ash, which turned Mei long into a fossil.

? True or false?

1. Swans can sleep standing on one leg.

2. Mei long means "tired lizard" in Chinese.

3. Scientists discovered Mei long's fossil in 2006.

See pages 130–131 for the answers.

Could dinosaurs smell better than dogs?

Dogs are champion sniffers, but Tyrannosaurus rex could have given them a run for their money. Some scientists think that the "tyrant lizard" had a sense of smell among the best of the meat-eating dinosaurs.

T. rex's powerful sense of smell may have let it track down prey at night.

Nostrils
Smells entered T. rex's nostrils, where they were picked up by receptors in the nasal cavity. The receptors then sent signals to the brain about the smells.

Tyrannosaurus rex
Some scientists think Tyrannosaurus rex used its keen sense of smell to scavenge, or find dead animals to eat, as well as to track and ambush prey.

? True or false?

1. The olfactory bulb is involved in hearing.

2. T. rex may have used its sense of smell to find prey.

3. Bloodhounds have a better sense of smell than humans.

See pages 130–131 for the answers.

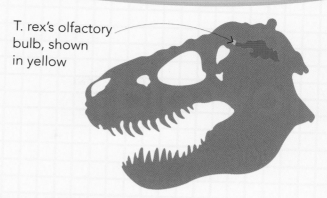

T. rex's olfactory bulb, shown in yellow

The brain and smell

Scientists can guess how big T. rex's brain was by the size of its skull. By studying birds, they can also get an idea about the size of its olfactory bulb. This is the part of the brain involved in smell. Scientists now think T. rex's olfactory bulb was quite big, which tells us that smell was its key sense.

Bloodhound

Bloodhounds are famous for tracking down humans and other animals by their scents. Scientists think this dog's sense of smell is 40 times sharper than ours.

Did dinosaurs grow old?

Dinosaurs went through many of the same life stages as humans as they grew, except they started life in hard-shelled eggs. Fossils found in the Gobi Desert in Asia show how Protoceratops changed over time.

Egg
Fossils show that Protoceratops took around 83 days (almost three months) to grow inside an egg. Dinosaur eggs had hard outer shells, similar to the shells of bird eggs.

Baby
As a baby, Protoceratops measured about 4–6 in (10–15 cm) long. To escape from the tough eggs, hatchlings may have had an egg tooth on their beaks, as some birds and reptiles do today, to help chip their way out.

Age determination
Dinosaur bones grew in a similar way to trees—in rings. Every year, another layer of bone would be added, so scientists can figure out a dinosaur's age when it died simply by counting the rings.

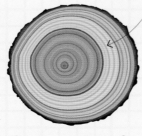

Every year, a tree grows another ring.

Cross-section of a tree trunk

Scientists can count the layers in a dinosaur bone to figure out its age.

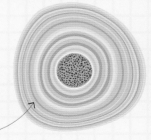

Cross-section of a dinosaur bone

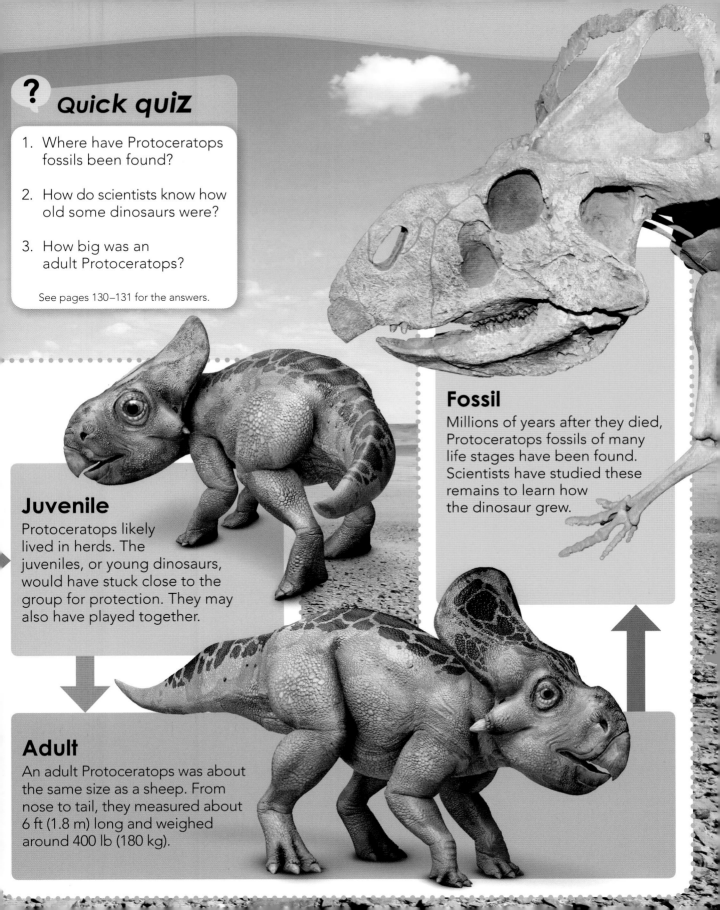

? Quick quiz

1. Where have Protoceratops fossils been found?

2. How do scientists know how old some dinosaurs were?

3. How big was an adult Protoceratops?

See pages 130–131 for the answers.

Fossil

Millions of years after they died, Protoceratops fossils of many life stages have been found. Scientists have studied these remains to learn how the dinosaur grew.

Juvenile

Protoceratops likely lived in herds. The juveniles, or young dinosaurs, would have stuck close to the group for protection. They may also have played together.

Adult

An adult Protoceratops was about the same size as a sheep. From nose to tail, they measured about 6 ft (1.8 m) long and weighed around 400 lb (180 kg).

Which dinosaur was the deadliest?

With their powerful jaws, razor-sharp claws, and fast bodies, theropods were one of the deadliest dinosaur groups. Some theropods hunted in packs, while others could take down large prey alone.

Limaysaurus

Allosaurus was the older cousin of the fearsome Tyrannosaurus rex.

How did theropods kill their prey?

Deinonychus

Deinonychus outnumbered their prey by hunting in packs. Using their curved toe claws as hooks, Deinonychus could hold on to prey animals while they struggled.

Allosaurus

These theropods had long, powerful arms. Allosaurus used their arms to catch and kill huge prey and were so strong that they could do this by themselves.

Giganotosaurus

Teeth

Theropod teeth were as sharp as knives and may have been able to shred dinosaur flesh to ribbons.

Claws

Theropods had two, three, or four fingers with sharp claws and also had claws on their toes. They used these to handle their prey.

? Quick quiz

1. Which dinosaur had the longest claws?

2. Which dinosaur had the most teeth?

3. Which dinosaur is the older cousin of T. rex?

See pages 130–131 for the answers.

The end of the dinosaurs

Some 66 million years ago, a huge meteorite crashed into Earth, triggering the death of the dinosaurs. The asteroid impact wiped out two-thirds of all species on Earth.

What happened to the dinosaurs?

Sixty-six million years ago, the dinosaurs died out when a huge meteorite hit Earth. The dinosaurs could not survive the changes that it caused.

Around 75 percent of all plant and animal species on Earth died out at the same time as the dinosaurs.

Starving dinosaurs

Hot debris from the asteroid started fires in America that destroyed vegetation. Without plants, plant-eating dinosaurs starved to death. This meant that the meat eaters eventually had no food either and so starved to death, too.

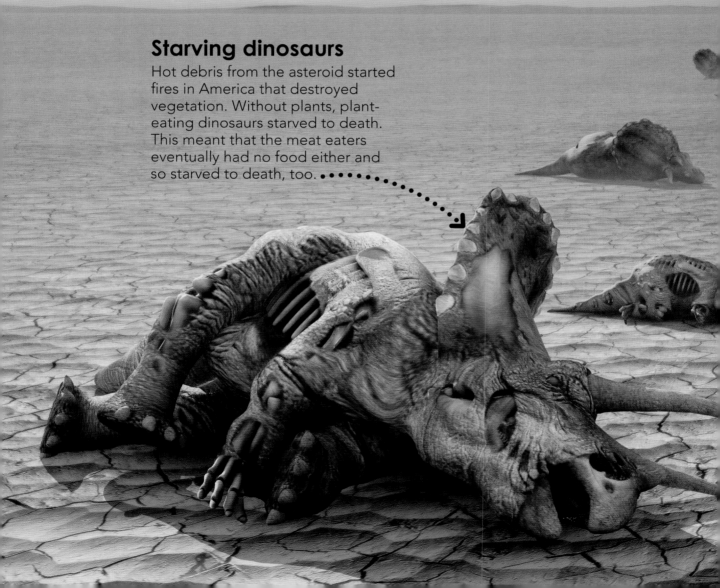

Dusty sky

Huge clouds of dust were thrown up into the sky when the meteorite hit the ground. Many plants and animal species suffered without sunlight.

See pages 130–131 for the answers.

? Quick quiz

1. When did the dinosaurs die out?

2. Around what percentage of plant and animal species survived?

3. Why did meat-eating dinosaurs starve?

Barren desert

Dust from the sky blocked out the sunlight needed for plants to grow. The land slowly turned into a desert.

How were dinosaurs wiped out?

Meteorite

Many scientists believe that a meteorite (a giant rock from space) hit Earth, which wiped out the dinosaurs. They think that this meteorite struck Earth at a massive speed of 62,000 mph (100,000 kph).

Tsunami

The meteorite that hit Earth may have caused a tsunami (a giant wave). This tsunami would have destroyed dinosaur homes and contributed to the extinction of the dinosaurs that were near it.

Did volcanoes kill the dinosaurs?

Scientists disagree about whether the dinosaurs died out 66 million years ago because of a giant asteroid smashing into Mexico's Yucatan Peninsula or because of a huge volcanic eruption. Most favor the asteroid strike, but there is some evidence that volcanic activity also played a part.

Temperature

Gases from the eruption could have been the trigger for climate changes that warmed and cooled the Earth. This would have been disastrous for life.

Which is the biggest active volcano?

The largest active volcano is Hawaii's Mauna Loa. It is more than 13,680 ft (4,170 m) high. Since 1843, Mauna Loa has erupted 33 times, most recently in 1984.

Deccan Traps

The Deccan Traps are a huge volcanic area where mass eruptions occurred at the end of the dinosaur era. They are in India. However, the world looked very different at the time.

The Deccan Traps

Ash and dust

A massive volcanic eruption spewed toxic gases into the sky and buried huge areas of land under ash and lava.

Lava

Giant volcanic eruptions caused lava to flow out more than 300 miles (480 km) from the volcano.

? Quick quiz

1. Where on Earth did the giant asteroid hit?

2. How hot is lava?

3. What could have caused climate change after the mass extinction event?

See pages 130–131 for the answers.

What animals survived?

The extinction event that caused the death of the dinosaurs also wiped out more than 70 percent of all species on the planet. Yet, life persisted. Many animals survived the destruction of the Cretaceous period, and we still see their relatives today.

Tuatara

Red-eyed tree frog

Reptiles

Reptiles such as tuataras managed to survive the extinction, but many other species of reptile did not make it.

Amphibians

Frogs and other amphibians, which live both in the water and on land, survived the extinction. Their small size may have meant they could hide from predators.

? *Quick quiz*

1. How many species are alive today?

2. Did mammals live alongside dinosaurs?

3. Did any dinosaurs survive the extinction?

See pages 130–131 for the answers.

Birds

No pterosaurs survived the extinction, but some bird species did, leaving these dinosaur descendants to become the new rulers of the sky.

Scarlet ibis

Possum

Greenland shark

Mammals

For millions of years, mammals lived in the shadows of dinosaurs, many coming out only at night. When the dinosaurs died out, mammals evolved to fill the dinosaurs' roles.

Which animals thrived after the dinosaurs?

Coryphodon

Once the dinosaurs died out, mammals such as Coryphodon could flourish and grow to huge sizes.

Creodont

Mammals such as creodonts rose to the top of the food chain to become fearsome predators.

Fish

Sea-dwelling plesiosaurs and mosasaurs disappeared with the dinosaurs, but fish deep below the surface survived.

Triceratops

Plant-eating Triceratops lived in North America, close to where the meteorite hit. Dinosaurs living near the site would have been affected first. The dust clouds caused by the meteorite blocked out the sun and made it difficult for plants to grow, which in turn meant that herbivores like Triceratops starved without food to eat.

T. rex

Even this top predator was not strong enough to survive the effects of the meteorite. Meat eaters like T. rex had their source of food cut off when herbivores such as Triceratops died off. This caused T. rex to die out.

Which dinosaurs died out when the meteorite hit?

When the meteorite slammed into what is now Mexico, it destroyed more than half of life on Earth. Some of the best-known dinosaurs were alive at the time of the impact, at the end of the Cretaceous period, including T. rex and Triceratops.

? True or false?

1. Therizinosaurus died out before Triceratops.

2. Brachiosaurus had already died out before the meteorite hit Earth.

3. The meteorite hit Mongolia.

See pages 130–131 for the answers.

Therizinosaurus

This dinosaur was one of the largest and last dinosaurs to live on Earth. It lived far from the location of the meteorite disaster—in what is now Mongolia. It would have taken longer for dinosaurs that lived farther away from the impact site to die out, but eventually they too met their end.

Some scientists think dinosaurs were already dying out at the end of the Cretaceous period.

Had any dinosaurs already died out before the extinction?

Brachiosaurus

This towering dinosaur, beloved by many dinosaur fans, lived between about 156 and 145 million years ago, during the Late Jurassic period. It went extinct long before the meteorite hit 66 million years ago.

Stegosaurus

Stegosaurus lived around 156 to 151 million years ago, during the Late Jurassic period. In fact, you are closer in time to T. rex—which lived 67 to 66 million years ago—than T. rex was to Stegosaurus!

Could I have a pet dinosaur?

You might already—if you own a pet bird! However, of the long-extinct dinosaurs, the dog-sized Psittacosaurus probably would have been a fun pet. Not only was it an herbivore— so it wouldn't eat you—it was also very cute!

? True or false?

1. Psittacosaurus was a carnivore.

2. Psittacosaurus had feathers.

3. Many dinosaurs became extinct due to the actions of humans.

See pages 130–131 for the answers.

Would dinosaurs survive in the modern world?

Food

If dinosaurs were our pets, we'd need to give them a variety of foods—just as we do for dogs and cats. Herbivorous pet dinosaurs could be given leaves and fruits, and carnivores would need plenty of meat.

Environment

The environment, or natural world, is under threat from pollution and habitat loss caused by humans. If dinosaurs were still around, they'd have the same problems as today's wild animals, and many would be facing extinction.

Large beak

Psittacosaurus had a large beak, which it used to crush nuts and chomp on thick-stemmed plants. It also swallowed stones to help it digest, or break down, tough food.

On a leash

Psittacosaurus is thought to have been a fast dinosaur. So you would have to keep a firm grip on its leash if you took it for a walk!

Psittacosaurus

This dinosaur's name means "parrot lizard," because it had a beak and quill-like feathers. It also had a large brain, so it may have been clever, like a dog.

Dinosaur discovery

Countless dinosaur species are buried around the world waiting to be discovered. With help from new high-tech tools, scientists are learning more and more about these fearsome beasts that once ruled the world.

What are fossils?

Fossils are the traces or remains of things that have been dead for millions of years. All kinds of life-forms have fossilized, from spectacular Stegosaurus skeletons to minuscule ammonite shells. Fossils help us understand how life on our planet has changed over millions and billions of years.

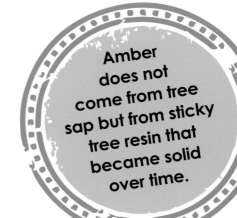

Amber does not come from tree sap but from sticky tree resin that became solid over time.

Ancient shell fossil

Ammonites fossilized in limestone

Mold fossil

These form when an animal or plant gets covered with mud, sand, and sediments after it dies. Over time, these substances harden. When the body or plant rots away, its impression is left behind.

Cast fossil

A cast is like the other half of a mold fossil. It occurs when water and minerals squeeze into a mold fossil and solidify, creating a three-dimensional shape that matches the shape of the dead plant or animal.

What was the first fossil ever found?

The first dinosaur fossil to be named was this Megalosaurus jawbone. William Buckland wrote about it in 1824. Richard Owen then came up with the term "dinosauria."

? Quick quiz

1. Does fossilized amber come from tree sap?

2. How old are the oldest fossils ever found?

3. What are trace fossils?

See pages 130–131 for the answers.

Dinosaur skull

Scorpion preserved in amber

Dinosaur footprint

Replacement fossil

These fossils form when minerals (naturally occurring solids) replace the original hard parts—including bones, shells, and leaves—of the dead animal or plant.

Body preservation

These are not fossils but are the original and unaltered animal bodies preserved in ice or amber. Examples include frozen mammoths and insects "trapped" in amber.

Trace fossil

Sometimes the only evidence of something's existence are the traces left behind, such as a footprint, scratch mark, or even its poop. These trace fossils show what dinosaurs ate, where they lived, and how they moved.

How are fossils formed?

Fossils are formed when a living thing, such as a dinosaur, dies, and its remains are buried. Over millions of years, the hard parts of its body, such as the bones, and sometimes softer body parts, turn into rock, creating fossils.

We only know that dinosaurs existed because of their fossil remains.

A dead Parasaurolophus sank to the bottom of the lake.

The softer parts of the body rotted away, leaving the skeleton.

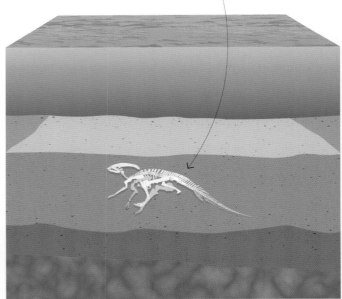

Death

Many of the best fossils come from dinosaurs that died in lakes, such as this Parasaurolophus. Their bodies sank to the bottom and were left undisturbed by scavengers that might otherwise have torn them apart.

Decay

The flesh fell off the Parasaurolophus's body as it decayed, or rotted. Eventually, all that remained of the animal were its bones. They were then covered in sediment—tiny pieces of rock and plant and animal material that sank to the lake bed.

? Quick quiz

1. How do dinosaur bones turn into rock?
   a) Minerals seep into them
   b) Lava replaces the bones
   c) They listen to too much rock music

2. How old is the earliest known dinosaur fossil?
   a) 3.5 billion years old
   b) 231 million years old
   c) 66 million years old

See pages 130–131 for the answers.

Which is the best-preserved fossil that's ever been found?

A contender for the most well-preserved fossil is a 110-million-year-old fossil of a nodosaur in the Royal Tyrrell Museum, Canada, which is so well preserved that it looks like it's still alive and ready for battle! Thanks to a rapid undersea burial, we can still see the details in the armored skin and spikes of this plant-eating dinosaur.

Layer upon layer of sediment built up, covering, preserving, and hardening the bones.

As rock layers wear away, the fossil skeleton comes to the surface.

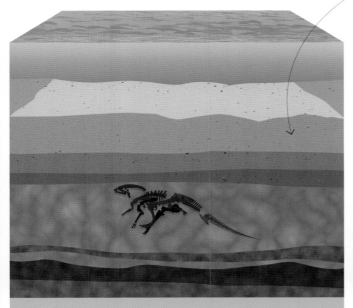

Sedimentation

Over millions of years, more layers of sediment piled up on top of the skeleton. Newer layers pressed down on deeper layers, which gradually turned into rock. Minerals seeped into the dinosaur's bones, too, and they also became rock.

Discovery

The lake bed was gradually pushed above sea level by the movement of the Earth's crust. Rock layers in the ground naturally wear away to reveal fossils. Fossil hunters can use tools to free the bones from the surrounding rock and display them for others to see and study.

Could I find a fossil in my backyard?

Fossilized remains of creatures that lived millions of years ago are hiding all over the world—in beaches, quarries, and maybe even in your backyard! There's only one way to find out...

Rock formation

Paleontologists have found the remains of aquatic animals that used to live in an inland sea in rocks across Utah.

Prehistoric fish

Garden

While clearing out a garden in Somerset, Britain, a woman stumbled across a fossilized seashell from 65 million years ago that belonged to an ammonite.

Ammonite

Has a child ever found a fossil?

Diego Suarez, a seven-year-old boy from Chile, discovered the bones of a strange beaked dinosaur in 2004 while exploring the Andes Mountains with his parents. Scientists named the new dinosaur Chilesaurus diegosuarezi. The family tree of Diego's dinosaur is uncertain, but scientists think it ate only plants.

? Quick quiz

1. What is an ammonite?

2. What dinosaur did Diego Suarez discover?

3. In what year was the fossil of a nodosaur found in Canada?

See pages 130–131 for the answers.

Quarry

Nodosaur

A miner discovered a complete fossil of a nodosaur, an armored dinosaur, while digging at a mine in Alberta, Canada, in 2011.

Beach

Ichthyosaur

The cliffs at Charmouth Beach on Britain's Jurassic Coast are teeming with fossils of long-gone marine animals.

Where have fossils been found?

Dinosaurs once roamed the planet. Their fossilized remains have been found on every continent. Fossils of other animals, including ancient humans, are also spread across the globe.

United States

In South Dakota lies the Hell Creek Formation, where masses of fossils have been found, including this 66-million-year-old Triceratops skull.

Argentina

Southern Argentina was the land of giants. Fossils of titanosaurs, the largest creatures to ever walk the planet, have been found here.

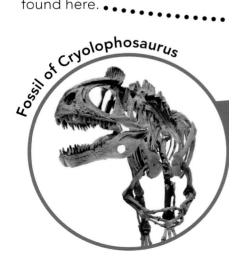

Fossil of Cryolophosaurus

Antarctica

Antarctica was once green and teeming with life. Cryolophosaurus prowled there during the Jurassic period.

Germany

The most famous feathered dinosaur fossil, Archaeopteryx, was found in Germany.

Fossilized oviraptorosaur eggs

China

In 1992, a farmer found four oviraptorosaur eggs in Nanyang, China. The species was named Beibeilong sinensis, which means "baby dragon from China."

Richmond pliosaur fossil

Australia

Remnants of marine reptiles, like ichthyosaurs and plesiosaurs, from the ancient Eromanga Sea can be found all across this continent.

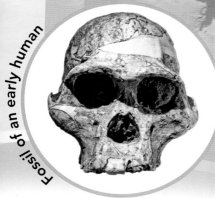

Fossil of an early human

South Africa

The site known as the "Cradle of Humankind" in South Africa is where the oldest human fossils have been found. In 1947, a 2.3-million-year-old skull was discovered.

? Quick quiz

1. Have dinosaur fossils been found in Antarctica?

2. Where have the oldest human fossils been found?

3. What does Beibeilong sinensis mean?

See pages 130–131 for the answers.

What is a paleontologist?

Paleontologists are scientists who study dinosaurs, prehistoric life, and fossilized remains. They use fossils to learn as much as possible about the ancient world and what lived in it millions and billions of years ago.

? Quick quiz

1. What tools do paleontologists use?

2. How long does it take to dig up a dinosaur skeleton?

3. What ancient fossilized animal was Mary Anning most famous for finding?

See pages 130–131 for the answers.

Fossil site
Dozens of paleontologists work together to dig up fossils. Digs require specialized equipment and can last for months.

Toolbox

Paleontologists need many tools to carefully unearth fossils. Drills and chisels are used to free the fossils from their rocky beds, while brushes are used to wipe away dust and dirt.

Mask

Chisels, hammer, and brushes

A paleontologist's tools

At work

Paleontologists clear away the rock and mud from each fossil. They must work very slowly and carefully.

Are there any famous paleontologists?

Mary Anning
One of the first fossil hunters, Mary Anning, discovered the famous long-necked plesiosaur.

Georges Cuvier
This French scientist helped show that species can go extinct and that pterosaurs were flying reptiles.

Jack Horner
Jack Horner discovered Maiasaura. He is best known for his work bringing dinosaurs to life in the movie *Jurassic Park*.

Removing bone

Using a combination of tools like big power drills and tiny dental picks, scientists are able to remove dinosaur bones from the earth. They dig a trench around the bones, then wrap them in plaster to protect them.

Moving the cast

Paleontologists need to carefully move the dinosaur bones, so they can be worked on by specialists in a lab. This might mean moving the bones with rope and a crane.

Is it easy to put a dinosaur back together?

Have you ever wondered how dinosaur bones end up on display at museums? Piecing a dinosaur together bone by bone is delicate work that can take paleontologists years to complete.

Cleaning

Paleontologists clean the fossils using tools such as picks, brushes, and special machines that are like miniature jackhammers.

How much are fossils worth?

Giraffatitan

This giant dinosaur is priceless, but when it and the other fossils around it were given a makeover in 2007, it cost the Museum für Naturkunde in Berlin, Germany, 18 million euros, or 20 million dollars.

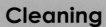

It took seven years to prepare the Apatosaurus fossil at the American Museum of Natural History in New York City.

Putting on display

Once they are ready, the fossils can be put on display in museums. They are sometimes positioned to show how they might have looked in a real-life situation: for instance, attacking prey.

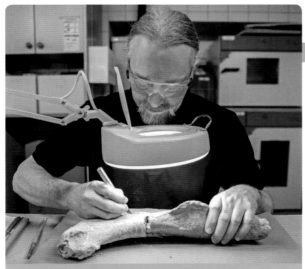

Repairing

Experts use a special glue or solution to repair and strengthen the bones. They also sculpt missing pieces out of putty or clay or produce them using a 3-D printer.

? Quick quiz

1. What tools are used to clean fossils?

2. What is wrapped around fossils to protect them?

3. How many good skeletons of dinosaurs have been found?

See pages 130–131 for the answers.

Did dinosaurs leave behind footprints?

Dinosaurs trampled across the Mesozoic world, and some of their footprints have been left behind as fossils. These fossils can tell us whether a dinosaur was big or small, fast or slow, and if it moved around in a herd or on its own.

Herd

Many similar footprints close together suggest that a group of dinosaurs was traveling in a herd.

Dinosaur tracks

Paleontologists study dinosaur footprints closely. They can figure out which type of dinosaur made a print by looking at the toes and the spacing between the footprints. These are probably theropod tracks.

Which is the biggest dinosaur footprint?

The largest known dinosaur footprint is about 5.5 ft (1.7 m) long—about as long as a refrigerator is high. The footprint belongs to a giant sauropod that stomped around what is now Australia about 130 million years ago.

? Quick quiz

1. What shape were theropod footprints?

2. How can you tell if dinosaurs were traveling in a herd?

3. How many dinosaur footprints have been found?

See pages 130–131 for the answers.

Distance

The distance between two footprints in a set can show how a dinosaur walked, and sometimes how fast it moved.

Types of footprint

Ornithopods had three toes that they put weight on while they walked, leaving a U-shaped footprint.

Sauropods put a lot of weight on their feet, making deep tracks. Their footprints usually look like massive blobs.

Theropods had three long, slim toes with pointy claws. They made V-shaped footprints.

Are birds dinosaurs?

Yes! Birds are the close relatives of theropod dinosaurs—the group that includes Deinonychus, Velociraptor, and Microraptor. They appeared in the Jurassic period and are the only dinosaurs to have survived the mass extinction event 66 million years ago.

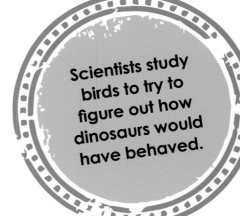

Scientists study birds to try to figure out how dinosaurs would have behaved.

Hollow bones

Modern birds have hollow bones, which make them light enough to fly. Theropod dinosaurs, such as Deinonychus, also had hollow bones.

A hollow bird bone

Microraptor

Microraptors were flying, non-bird dinosaurs. They had four wings, with the second set on their legs.

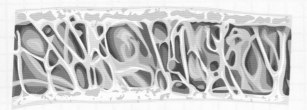

Deinonychus

This ferocious feathered raptor was one of the dinosaurs that inspired scientists to suggest a link with birds.

Deinonychus had feathers but could not fly.

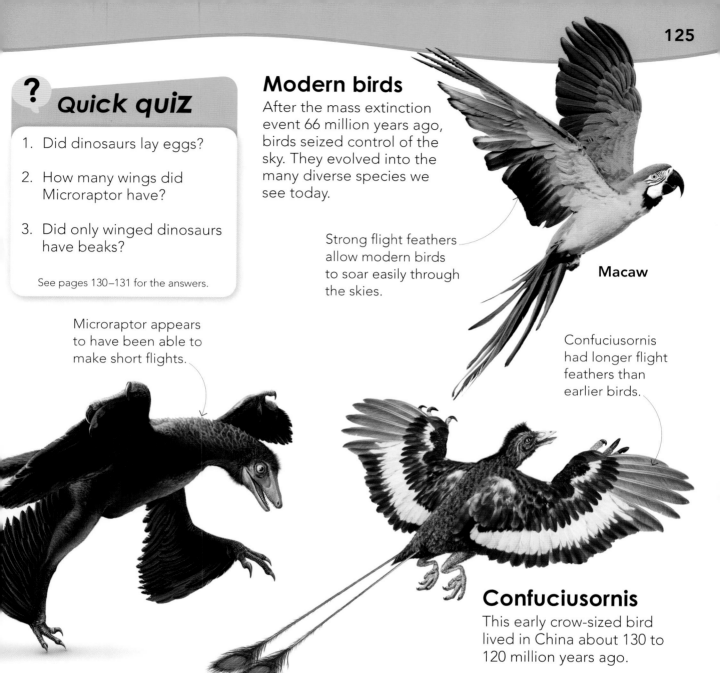

? Quick quiz

1. Did dinosaurs lay eggs?

2. How many wings did Microraptor have?

3. Did only winged dinosaurs have beaks?

See pages 130–131 for the answers.

Modern birds

After the mass extinction event 66 million years ago, birds seized control of the sky. They evolved into the many diverse species we see today.

Strong flight feathers allow modern birds to soar easily through the skies.

Macaw

Microraptor appears to have been able to make short flights.

Confuciusornis had longer flight feathers than earlier birds.

Confuciusornis

This early crow-sized bird lived in China about 130 to 120 million years ago.

Did dinosaurs have beaks?

Ichthyornis

This 90-million-year-old seabird was about the size of a gull. It had a beak with sharp, dinosaur-like teeth, which it used to catch small, slippery fish.

Psittacosaurus

Known as the "parrot lizard," this four-legged dinosaur had a birdlike beak that it used to crush and cut thick plants. However, it was not a bird.

What can we learn from dinosaur poop?

It's not just the body parts of dinosaurs that can become fossils—their poop can, too! These fossils are called coprolites, and they give us a firsthand look at what dinosaurs ate. All kinds of things have been found in coprolites, including tree bark, seeds, bits of bone, and shells.

Coprolite

A coprolite forms just like other fossils. Recently produced poop gets covered up and, over millions of years, turns into hard minerals.

Plants

Sometimes scientists find tree bark, seeds, or pollen in a coprolite. This tells them that the dinosaur was a plant eater or included plants in its diet.

Bones

Coprolites from meat eaters contain fragments of bone. Sometimes teeth marks can even be seen in the fragments.

Can you find coprolites in the sea?

Ichthyosaur
Ichthyosaurs liked to chew on squid-like creatures called belemnites. We know this because an ichthyosaur coprolite was found containing more than 200 cone-shaped belemnite shells.

Sea turtle
This poop from a Cretaceous-period sea turtle contains clam-like mollusks with thin shells. Prehistoric sharks also left behind coprolites, which are spiral-shaped.

The largest coprolite found so far is 17 in (44 cm) long! It's full of bits of bone and probably came from a T. rex.

Parasites
Dinosaurs also had to deal with parasites—small animals that live inside them—such as tapeworms. Scientists have found tapeworm eggs inside coprolites.

? Quick quiz

1. What's another name for fossil poop?

2. Which dinosaur is thought to be responsible for the largest known coprolite?

3. How many coprolites are there in the largest coprolite collection?

See pages 130–131 for the answers.

Are we still finding out about dinosaurs?

About every ten days, scientists discover a new species of dinosaur. These days, they use special tools, such as scanners and ultraviolet light cameras, to get as much information as possible from dinosaur fossils.

Lasers can be used to reveal hidden features and sometimes the original colors of fossils.

3-D scanning

Researchers can use handheld 3-D scanners to create computer models of fossils, such as this Triceratops skull. They then study the models and can also share them with other scientists around the world.

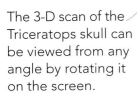

The 3-D scan of the Triceratops skull can be viewed from any angle by rotating it on the screen.

MRI scanning

MRI scanning uses radio waves to look inside an object. It can identify chemicals that were once part of dinosaurs.

This screen shows MRI scans of the fossil skull of a theropod called Arcovenator.

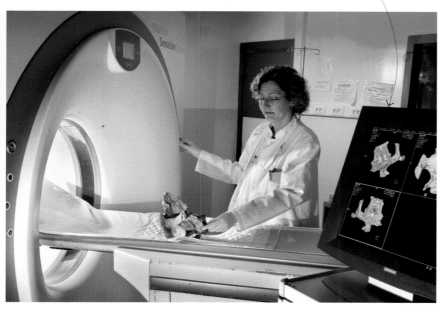

What dinosaurs have been discovered recently?

Dracorex hogwartsia
The "dragon king of Hogwarts" was given its name by *Harry Potter* fans. Its fossils were found in South Dakota.

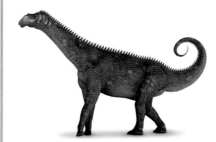

Mierasaurus
This North American sauropod may have had European ancestors that crossed a land bridge that once connected the continents.

Ultraviolet light

Ultraviolet light can reveal traces of colors in fossils. This gives us an idea of what ancient animals looked like when alive.

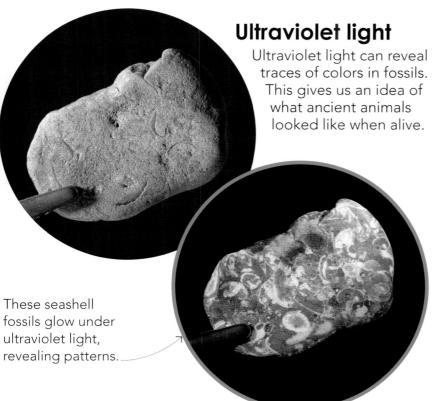

These seashell fossils glow under ultraviolet light, revealing patterns.

? *True or false?*

1. Scientists discover a new species of dinosaur about once a year.

2. 3-D scans of fossils help scientists learn more about dinosaurs.

3. Mierasaurus lived in Australia.

See pages 130–131 for the answers.

Answers

Page 9 1) They all have their legs positioned directly under their bodies and lay and hatch from eggs. 2) Richard Owen. 3) It means "king of the tyrant lizards."

Page 11 1) An asteroid hitting Earth. 2) Four. 3) A dinosaur called Nyasasaurus parringtoni.

Page 12 1) Yes, eventually they will drift together to make a new supercontinent. 2) Pangaea. 3) The Cretaceous period.

Page 14 1) Yes. 2) No, land has moved around and temperatures have changed. 3) No, they migrated in search of food.

Page 16 Sauropods.

Page 19 1) False. Dinosaurs lived long before humans existed. 2) True. 3) True.

Page 21 1) Pine nuts. 2) 145 to 66 million years ago. 3) It contained less oxygen and more carbon dioxide.

Page 23 1) The Loch Ness Monster. 2) 5.5 tons. 3) 76.

Page 25 1) Spiky leaves. 2) 360 million years ago. 3) "Living fossils."

Page 29 1) The same length as two school buses. 2) To dig for insects, hold on to prey, and defend themselves from enemies. 3) Bigger.

Page 31 1) Around 150 million years ago. 2) To keep them warm.

Page 32 1) False. They were the size of birds. 2) True. 3) True.

Page 34 1) Four chambers. 2) Yes. In 2015, researchers found the remains of red blood cells inside a dinosaur fossil. 3) 96.3°F (35.7°C).

Page 37 1) A second set of ribs in a dinosaur's belly that may have helped with breathing. 2) No. 3) Saurischia and Ornithischia.

Page 39 1) Patagotitan. 2) Whale. 3) Plants.

Page 41 Ostrich.

Page 42 1) They used spikes as weapons and to defend themselves against enemies. 2) Yes, they had plates on their eyelids to protect their eyes. 3) It had a heavy club at the end of its tail.

Page 44 1) In bird beaks and our fingernails. 2) About 6.5 ft (2 m) wide. 3) Many animals lock horns, including impalas, deer, goats, springbok, cows, water buffalo, moose, and wildebeests.

Page 47 1) In 2009. 2) The Epidexipteryx. 3) The Dromaeosauriformipes rarus.

Page 49 1) Omnivores. 2) Plants. 3) Plants and leaves.

Page 51 1) 10 in (25 cm) thick. 2) To draw the attention of mates. 3) Plants.

Page 53 1) a. 2) A carnivore.

Page 55 1) 60. 2) A velociraptor's. 3) Lighter.

Page 57 1) Sauropods, such as Diplodocus and Supersaurus. 2) Yes. 3) Sinosauropteryx.

Page 59 1) False. They have been found in Mongolia and China. 2) False. Most dinosaurs buried their eggs to protect them from predators. 3) True.

Page 60 1) c. 2) c.

Page 64 1) A sclerotic ring. 2) Carnivore. 3) Plants.

Page 66 1) No. 2) A larynx. 3) Elephants, tortoises, and horses.

Page 69 1) Crocodiles, alligators, and birds. 2) Oviraptor. 3) They could be hundreds.

Page 71 1) Cryolophosaurus. 2) No, their feathers tend to be brown, gray, or cream.

Page 73 1) T. rex. 2) A sail. 3) No, Spinosaurus was extinct by the time T. rex appeared. They also lived in different places.

Page 75 1) Trapping and spearing fish. 2) Yes. 3) A crocodile.

Page 77 1) To avoid being attacked by predators. 2) A pride. 3) Omnivores.

Page 79 1) They were lightweight and hollow. 2) Flap their wings. 3) About the size of songbirds, such as a blackbird or bluebird.

Page 80 1) Carnivorous dinosaurs could open their mouths wider. 2) Between 11 and 25 mph (17 and 40 kph).

Page 83 Troodon.

Page 85 1) A form of camouflage where an animal has a darker upper body and lighter underside. 2) Gray, black, and white. 3) Sinosauropteryx.

Page 87 1) Around the same size as a crow. 2) Flying squirrels and flying dragons. 3) China.

Page 89 1) True. 2) False. It means "soundly sleeping dragon." 3) False. It was discovered in 2004.

Page 91 1) False. It is involved in smell. 2) True. 3) True.

Page 93 1) The Gobi Desert, Asia. 2) From counting the layers of bone in a dinosaur fossil. 3) 6 ft (1.8 m) from top to tail.

Page 95 1) Therizinosaurus. 2) Hadrosaur. 3) Allosaurus.

Page 99 1) 66 million years ago. 2) Around 25 percent. 3) Because the plant-eating dinosaurs died, so there were no other dinosaurs to eat.

Page 101 1) Yucatan Peninsula, Mexico. 2) Lava has been found to get as hot as 1,600°F (871°C). 3) Gases from the eruption.

Page 102 1) As many as 10,000. 2) Yes, for millions of years. 3) Yes, birds did.

Page 104 1) False. Triceratops lived close to where the meteorite hit so would have probably died before Therizinosaurus. 2) True. 3) False. It hit in Mexico.

Page 106 1) False. It was an herbivore. 2) True. 3) False. Dinosaurs died out many millions of years before humans evolved.

Page 111 1) No, it comes from tree resin. 2) Around 3.5 billion years old. 3) Fossils that have been produced by an organism in some way, such as footprints or poop.

Page 113 1) a. 2) b.

Page 115 1) An extinct ancient shellfish. 2) The Chilesaurus diegosuarezi. 3) 2011.

Page 117 1) Yes. 2) The Cradle of Humankind, South Africa. 3) "Baby dragon from China."

Page 118 1) Brushes, chisels, and drills. 2) It depends! Anything from hours to years. 3) The long-necked plesiosaur.

Page 121 1) Brushes and dental tools. 2) Plaster. 3) It has been estimated to be around 2,100.

Page 123 1) V-shaped. 2) They left many similar footprints, close together. 3) Hundreds of thousands.

Page 125 1) Yes. 2) Four. 3) No, Psittacosaurus had a beak and no wings.

Page 127 1) Coprolite. 2) T. rex. 3) More than 1,200 coprolites.

Page 129 1) False. Currently, scientists find about one every ten days. 2) True. 3) False. It lived in North America.

Quiz your friends!

Who knows the most about dinosaurs? Test your friends and family with these tricky questions. See pages 134–135 for the answers.

Questions

1. Which was the **tallest dinosaur**?

5. How big is the **largest dinosaur coprolite** (fossilized poop)?

8. Which was the **spikiest dinosaur**?

10. How far did **dinosaurs travel**?

2. Did dinosaurs make **nests**?

3. What is the **name** for a **scientist** who looks for dinosaurs?

4. Where did most of the **dinosaurs live**?

7. Did dinosaurs meet mammoths?

6. Which dinosaur had the **biggest horns**?

9. Did dinosaurs fight?

11. What is the name for the types of dinosaurs that **ate only meat**?

13. How many **legs** did **dinosaurs walk** on?

14. Were **dinosaurs brightly** colored?

12. Which dinosaur had the **biggest feet**?

15. Which dinosaur was the **first to be discovered**?

Answers

1. Probably Sauroposeidon, at **60 ft (18.5 m) tall**

8. Probably **Kentrosaurus,** which had **two rows of spikes** down its back

7. **No**—they lived during different times

9. **Yes! Meat-eating dinosaurs hunted other dinosaurs,** and dinosaurs probably fought others of their own species

2. **Yes**

3. A paleontologist

4. **Dinosaur fossils** have been **found** all over the world, but the best places to find them are **China**, **Argentina**, and **North America**

5. **17 in (44 cm) long!**

6. **Coahuilaceratops**, related to Triceratops, **had horns** that were **4 ft (1.2 m) long**

10. The **largest dinosaurs migrated** seasonally, covering hundreds of miles

11. **Carnivores**

12. An unknown **species of sauropod** dinosaur, with **footprints 5.5 ft (1.7 m) long**

13. Some on **two feet**, some on **four**

14. **It's impossible to know for sure. Some paleontologists say they were, because** birds are closely related to dinosaurs

15. **Megalosaurus**

Dinosaur names

Dinosaur and other prehistoric animal names can be tricky! Here's a list showing how to pronounce them.

A

Acrotholus	ACK-roe-THO-luss
Arcovenator	are-COE-ven-ah-tore
Albertonectes	al-BERT-oh-nek-teez
Albertosaurus	al-BERT-oh-SORE-us
Allosaurus	AL-oh-SORE-us
Alxasaurus	ALK-sah-SORE-us
Anchiornis	AN-kee-OR-niss
Ankylosaurus	ANK-ill-oh-SORE-us
Apatosaurus	a-PAT-oh-SORE-us
Archaeopteryx	ar-kee-OP-ter-ix
Argentinosaurus	ARE-jen-TEEN-oh-SORE-us

B

Baryonyx	bah-ree-ON-ix
Beibeilong sinensis	bay-bay-long si-nen-sis
Brachiosaurus	brackee-oh-SORE-us

C

Camarasaurus	KAM-a-ra-SORE-us
Carnotaurus	car-noe-TOR-us
Caudipteryx	caw-DIP-ter-ix
Chilesaurus	chi-le-SORE-us
diegosuarezi	dee-egg-oh-SW-are-EZ-i
Chiniquodon	chin-ik-oo-oh-don
Citipati	SIH-tee-PAH-tee
Coelophysis	SEE-low-FYE-sis
Compsognathus	COMP-sog-NAITH-us
Confuciusornis	con-FEW-shus-OR-niss
Corythosaurus	ko-RITH-oh-SORE-us
Cryolophosaurus	cry-o-LOAF-o-SORE-us

D

Deinonychus	dye-NON-ee-cus
Dimetrodon	die-MET-roe-don
Diplodocus	dip-LOD-oh-kus
Dracorex	DRAK-o-rex
Dreadnoughtus	dred-NOOR-tuss
Dromaeosauri -formipes rarus	DRO-me-oh-SORE-ih-FORM-ih-pes rare-us

E

Edmontosaurus	ed-MONT-oh-SORE-us
Elasmosaurus	el-LAZZ-moe-SORE-us
Eoraptor	EE-oh-rap-tor
Epidexipteryx	ep-EE-dex-ip-TER-ix
Erlikosaurus	er-lik-oh-SORE-us
Euoplocephalus	YOU-owe-plo-SEFF-ah-lus

G

Gallimimus	GAL-ih-MIME-us
Giganotosaurus	gig-AN-oh-toe-SORE-us
Giraffatitan	ji-RAF-a-TIE-tan
Guanlong	GWON-long

H

Hadrosaurus	HAD-roh-SORE-us
Halszkaraptor	hals-ka-RAP-tor
Herrerasaurus	heh-RARE-ra-SORE-uss

I

Ichthyornis	ICK-thee-OR-niss
Ichthyosaurus	ICK-thee-oh-SORE-us
Iguanodon	ig-GWAH-no-don
Isanosaurus	ee-sahn-oh-SORE-us

K

Kentrosaurus	KEN-troh-SORE-us
Kosmoceratops	KOS-moe-SERRA-tops

L

Limaysaurus	lih-may-SORE-us
Linhenykus	LIN-huh-NYE-kuss
Liopleurodon	LIE-oh-PLOOR-oh-don
Lystrosaurus	LIS-trow-SORE-us

M

Magyarosaurus	mag-yar-oh-SORE-us
Maiasaura	MY-a-SORE-a
Megalosaurus	MEG-uh-lo-SORE-us
Megazostrodon	MEG-ah-ZO-stroh-don
Mei long	MAY long
Microraptor	MY-crow-RAP-tor
Mierasaurus	me-EHR-ah-SORE-us
Moros intrepidus	moh-ros in-treh-pi-dus
Mosasaurus	MOSE-ah-SORE-us
Muttaburrasaurus	MOO-tah-BUH-ruh-SORE-us

N

Nodosaur	NOD-oh-SORE

O

Ornithischian	OR-nith-is-kee-un
Ornithomimids	OR-nith-oh-mi-mids
Ouranosaurus	oo-RAN-oh-SORE-us
Oviraptor	OVE-ih-rap-tor

P

Pachyceph-alosaurus	PACK-ee-SEF-ah-low-SORE-us
Parasaurolophus	PA-ra-SORE-oh-LOAF-us
Patagotitan	pat-AG-oh-tie-tan
Pentaceratops	PEN-ta-SERRA-tops
Plateosaurus	PLATE-ee-oh-SORE-us
Pliosaur	plee-oh-sore
Protoceratops	PRO-toe-SERRA-tops
Psittacosaurus	si-tak-a-SORE-us
Pteranodon	teh-RAN-oh-don

S

Sauroposeidon	SORE-oh-pos-i-den
Shunosaurus	SHOE-noe-SORE-us
Sinosauropteryx	SIGH-no-sore-OP-ter-ix
Spinophorosaurus	SPINE-off-oh-ro-SORE-us
Spinosaurus	SPINE-oh-SORE-us
Stegosaurus	STEG-oh-SORE-us
Struthiomimus	STROO-thee-oh-MIME-us
Stygimoloch	STIJ-ee-moh-lok
Styracosaurus	sty-RACK-oh-SORE-us
Suchomimus	soo-ko-MIME-us

T

Tarbosaurus	TAR-bow-SORE-us
Therizinosaurus	THERRY-zin-oh-SORE-us
Thylacosmilus	THIGH-lah-coe-SMILE-us
Triceratops	try-SERRA-tops
Tupandactylus imperator	too-pan-DAK-til-us im-PEH-rah-tor
Tyrannosaurus rex	TIE-ran-oh-SORE-us rex

U

Uberabatitan	OO-ber-ah-bah-ty-tan
Uintatherium	WIN-tah-THEE-ree-um

V

Velociraptor	vel-OSS-ee-RAP-tor

Y

Yi qi	yee chee

Use this guide if you need help saying our names.

Glossary

ammonite
Extinct ancient shellfish that was alive in the Mesozoic era

amphibians
Group of cold-blooded animals that that live in water and can walk on land as adults

ancient
Something that is very old and existed a long time ago

ankylosaurs
Plant-eating, four-legged dinosaurs that had body armor, such as spikes and plates. They lived in the Cretaceous period

armor
Natural features, such as plates and spikes, that protect an animal from harm

camouflage
Patterns or colors on an animal's skin, feathers, or fur that make it blend in with its surroundings

carnivore
Animal that eats only meat

ceratopsians
Plant-eating, four-legged dinosaurs that have horns and beaks. They lived in the Jurassic and Cretaceous periods

climate
Weather and temperature of a place or during a period of time

coprolite
Animal poop that has become fossilized

Cretaceous period
Third, and last, period of the Mesozoic era. It occurred 145 to 66 million years ago

dinosaur
Dominant group of animals that lived on land during the Mesozoic Era

environment
Natural surroundings of a living thing

eruption
When lava, and sometimes ash and rocks, explode out of a volcano due to a buildup of pressure

evolve
Way living things change and adapt over time to help them survive

extinction
When a group, or species, of animals or plants has completely died out

forage
When animals search for food

fossil
Remains of plants or animals, such as dinosaurs, that died a long time ago and have been preserved in the Earth over time

fossilization
Process by which a plant or animal becomes a fossil

habitat
Place where an animal or plant lives

hadrosaurs
Group of dinosaurs with duck bills, and sometimes crests. They lived in the Cretaceous period

herbivore
Animal that eats only plants

herd
Group of animals that travel or live together

ichthyosaur
Type of marine reptile that was shaped like a dolphin and lived in the Mesozoic era

invertebrate
Animal without a backbone

Jurassic period
Second period of the Mesozoic era. It occurred 200 to 145 million years ago

mammals
Group of warm-blooded animals with fur or hair. This group includes dogs and bears

Mesozoic era
Triassic, Jurassic, and Cretaceous periods together

meteorite
Piece of rock or metal from space that collides with the Earth

omnivore
Animal that eats both plants and meat

ornithopods
Group of plant-eating dinosaurs that includes the hadrosaurs

pachycephalosaurs
Plant-eating or omnivorous dinosaurs with domed heads and two legs. They lived in the Cretaceous period

paleontologist
Scientist who studies fossils to understand the history of life on Earth

Pangaea
Name of the Earth's supercontinent from 335 to 175 million years ago

plesiosaur
Type of marine reptile that lived in the Mesozoic era

predator
Animal that hunts and kills other living animals for food

prehistoric
Ancient time that existed before information was written down

preserved
Way of making sure the remains of a plant or animal do not change much over time

prey
Animal that is hunted and killed by another animal for food

pterosaurs
Prehistoric flying reptiles of the Mesozoic era

remains
Body of a dead animal

reptiles
Group of four-limbed animals that lay eggs and live entirely on land. This group includes lizards, crocodiles, and snakes

sauropods
Plant-eating dinosaurs with four legs, long necks, and long tails. They lived in the Triassic, Jurassic, and Cretaceous periods

scavenger
Animal that feeds on the leftover meat of another dead animal

skeleton
Frame of bones in an animal's body that supports it and helps it move

species
Group of similar animals, or plants, that have the same features

stegosaurs
Plant-eating, four-legged dinosaurs with plates or spines down their backs. They lived in the Jurassic and Cretaceous periods

supercontinent
Area of land when all of the Earth's continents were joined together

territory
Area that an animal considers its own and that it will defend from other animals

theropods
Group of meat-eating, two-legged dinosaurs. They lived in the Triassic, Jurassic, and Cretaceous periods

tracks
Footprints or markings left by an animal as it moved through an area

Triassic period
First period of the Mesozoic era. It occurred 251 to 200 million years ago

vertebrae
Bones that form the spine of an animal or human

vertebrate
Animal with a backbone

Index

Acknowledgments

DORLING KINDERSLEY would like to thank: Caroline Hunt for proofreading; Helen Peters for the index; Abi Luscombe, Seeta Parmar, Becky Walsh, and Sam Priddy for editorial assistance; Emma Hobson, Fiona Macdonald, Elle Ward, Rashika Kachroo, and Kartik Gera for additional design; and Ashok Kumar and Nityanand Kumar for technical support.

Smithsonian Enterprises
Consultant Matthew T. Miller, Museum Specialist, Department of Paleobiology, National Museum of Natural History, Smithsonian
Product Development Manager Kealy Gordon
Senior Manager Licensed Publishing Ellen Nanney
Director, Licensed Publishing Jill Corcoran
Vice President, Consumer and Education Products Brigid Ferraro
President Carol LeBlanc

The publisher would like to thank the following for their kind permission to reproduce their photographs:

(Key: a-above; b-below/bottom; c-center; f-far; l-left; r-right; t-top)

1 Dorling Kindersley: Dan Crisp (cb). **2 Dorling Kindersley**: Jon Hughes (br). **3 Alamy Stock Photo**: Jim Lane (br). **Dorling Kindersley**: Dan Crisp (cra, bc). **4 Dorling Kindersley**: Dan Crisp (cra). **5 Science Photo Library**: Mikkel Juul Jensen (cb). **6 Alamy Stock Photo**: Stocktrek Images, Inc. **7 Dorling Kindersley**: Simon Mumford / Colorado Plateau Geosystems Inc. (ca). **8–9 Getty Images**: Mark Wilson / Newsmakers. **10 123RF.com**: Leonello Calvetti (cr). **Alamy Stock Photo**: Leonello Calvetti (br); Corey Ford (fcr). **Dreamstime.com**: Leonello Calvetti (clb); Corey A Ford (tr). **11 123RF.com**: Mark Turner (ca); Mark Turner (tc); Mark Turner (ca); Stocktrek Images, Inc. (ca/Chiniquodon). **Dreamstime.com**: Anphotos (bl); Nicolas Fernandez (c/Megazostrodon, br); Mr1805 (cb). **12 Dorling Kindersley**: Dan Crisp (cra, crb); Simon Mumford / Colorado Plateau Geosystems Inc. (c, cr). **13 Dorling Kindersley**: Dan Crisp (clb, ca, cb, crb); Simon Mumford / Colorado Plateau Geosystems Inc. (cl, c, cr). **16 Alamy Stock Photo**: MasPix (crb); **Science Photo Library** (clb). **Getty Images**: Yuriy Priymak / Stocktrek Images (cr). **16–17 iStockphoto.com**: Dottedhippo (t). **17 Alamy Stock Photo**: Stocktrek Images, Inc. (cl). **Science Photo Library**: Roger Harris (clb). **18 Dreamstime.com**: Adambowers (c); Elena Gladkaya (cr); Sippapas (fclb); Vaeenma (fcra, bl); Peter Minister and Andrew Kerr / Xunbin Pan (cl). **18–19 Dorling Kindersley**: Simon Mumford / Colorado Plateau Geosystems Inc. (c). **19 123RF.com**: Leonello Calvetti (tl); Corey A Ford (cla); Mark Turner (cb). **Alamy Stock Photo**: Stocktrek Images, Inc. (ca). **Dreamstime.com**: Elena Gladkaya (fcla, c, c/Mesozoic era trees, cb/Mesozoic era forest, crb); Mark Turner (cra). **Age Fotostock** (cb). **Dreamstime.com**: Iskandarov (bl); Markit (cb/Horsetail shoots). **20–21 Alamy Stock Photo**: MBI (b). James Kuether. **21 Getty Images**: Emily Willoughby / Stocktrek Images (crb). **22 Alamy Stock Photo**: MasPix (ca/Ichthyosaurus). **Dreamstime.com**: Paul Fleet (cla); Andreas Meyer (r). **Science Photo Library**: Jaime Chirinos (ca). **23 123RF.com**: Michael Rosskothen (cla). **Dorling Kindersley**: Jon Hughes (cr). **24 Dreamstime.com**: Yujie Chen (tr). **24–25 Dreamstime.com**: Carlos Restrepo (b). **25 Dorling Kindersley**: Natural History Museum, London (ca); Oxford Museum of Natural History (cra). **Dreamstime.com**: Radu Borcoman / Radukan (cr). **26 Alamy Stock Photo**: AGF Srl (cla); Mohamad Haghani (b). **27 Alamy Stock Photo**: MasPix (t). **28 Dorling Kindersley**: Jon Hughes (crb). **Dreamstime.com**: Mr1805 (bl). **iStockphoto.com**: Warpaintcobra (r). **29 Alamy Stock Photo**: Dan Barbatala (r). **30 Dorling Kindersley**: Senckenberg Nature Museum. **31 Dreamstime.com**: Gorshkov13 (ca); Martin Pelanek (cla); Ondrej Prosický (cra). **32 Dreamstime.com**: Mr1805 (clb). **32–33 Dreamstime.com**: Leonello Calvetti (cb). **33 123RF.com**: Michael Rosskothen (cla). **35 123RF.com**: Michael Rosskothen (crb). **Dreamstime.com**: Mr1805 (cr). **36 Dorling Kindersley**: Dan Crisp (cb, bc). **36–37 Dreamstime.com**: Leonello Calvetti. **37 123RF.com**: Mark Turner (cra). **38–39 Alamy Stock Photo**: Mohamad Haghani. **39 Dreamstime.com**: Mr1805 (cla). **40–41 Alamy Stock Photo**: Stocktrek Images, Inc. **41 123RF.com**: Alexis Bélec (cra). **42–43 Alamy Stock Photo**: MasPix. **43 Alamy Stock Photo**: Fresh Start Images (crb). **44–45 James Kuether (b). 44 Science Photo Library**: Susumu Nishinaga (cra). **45 Alamy Stock Photo**: Jean-Fr@Ncois Ducasse (cra); RooM the Agency (ca). **47 Alamy Stock Photo**: Steve Vidler (ca). **48 Getty Images**: Mohamad Haghani / Stocktrek Images (bl). **48–49 Alamy Stock Photo**: Stocktrek Images, Inc. (b). **49 Alamy Stock Photo**: Mohamad Haghani (br). **Science Photo Library**: Laurie O'keefe (ca). **50 Alamy Stock Photo**: Jim Lane (t). **51 Alamy Stock Photo**: Stocktrek Images, Inc. (cra). **Dorling Kindersley**: James Kuether (cra/Stygimoloch). **James Kuether**. **52–53 Alamy Stock Photo**: Mohamad Haghani. **iStockphoto.com**: OlgaPtashko (Background). **52 Alamy Stock Photo**: Corbin17 (crb). **53 Friends of North Carolina Museum of Natural Sciences**: Jorge Gonzalez (cr). **Science Photo Library**: Jose Antonio Penas (cra). **54–55 Alamy Stock Photo**: AGF Srl. **55 Alamy Stock Photo**: Stocktrek Images, Inc. (br). **56 Alamy Stock Photo**: Friedrich Saurer (br). **Dorling Kindersley**: Jon Hughes (bc). **iStockphoto.com**: Elenarts (clb). **56–57 iStockphoto.com**: CoreyFord (b). **57 Getty Images**: Feature China / Barcroft Images / Barcroft Media (cla); Mohamad Haghani / Stocktrek Images (cra). **iStockphoto.com**: Leonello (cb). **58 Alamy Stock Photo**: Natural Visions (cb). **Dorling Kindersley**: Dorset Dinosaur Museum. **Dreamstime.com**: Sergeyoch (fclb). **58–59 123RF.com**: Oleg Palii (b). **Dorling Kindersley**: Dorset Dinosaur Museum. **59 Alamy Stock Photo**: World History Archive (cb). **Dorling Kindersley**: Natural History Museum, London (crb). **Dreamstime.com**: Skypixel (clb). **James Kuether** (ca). **Science Photo Library**: Dirk Wiersma (cla). **60 Dreamstime.com**: Dragoneye (crb). **61 Alamy Stock Photo**: Q-Images (cla); Stocktrek Images, Inc. (cra). **Dreamstime.com**: Paulus Rusyanto (c). **Getty Images**: Nobumichi Tamura / Stocktrek Images (crb); Sergey Krasovskiy (cr). **62 Alamy Stock Photo**: Mohamad Haghani (br); Stocktrek Images, Inc. (cl). **64 Alamy Stock Photo**: Stocktrek Images, Inc. (cr). **64–65 Alamy Stock Photo**: Corey Ford (ca). **65 Dreamstime.com**: Andrey Armyagov (cl); Corey A Ford (clb); Zepherwind (cra). **66 Dreamstime.com**: Sebastian Kaulitzki (tl). **67 Alamy Stock Photo**: Ian Dagnall (br). **68 Alamy Stock Photo**: Science History Images (cra). **71 Dorling Kindersley**: Jon Hughes (bc). **Dreamstime.com**: Shawn Hempel (cra). **72 Alamy Stock Photo**: Leonello Calvetti (b). **73 Getty Images**: Sciepro (b). **74 Dorling Kindersley**: Peter Minister (clb). **74–75 Alamy Stock Photo**: Stocktrek Images, Inc. **76–77 Alamy Stock Photo**: Corey Ford. **77 123RF.com**: Thomas Samantzis (cla). **78 Alamy Stock Photo**: Stocktrek Images, Inc. (cb); YAY Media AS (cl). **78–79 Alamy Stock Photo**: Stocktrek Images, Inc. **79 Alamy Stock Photo**: Hans Winke (cra). **82 Science Photo Library**: Millard H. Sharp / Science Source (ca). **83 Alamy Stock Photo**: Leonello Calvetti (l). **84–85 Dreamstime.com**: Janina Kubik. **85 Alamy Stock Photo**: National Geographic Image Collection (bc). **86 Alamy Stock Photo**: Avalon / Photoshot License (clb); Nature Picture Library (cb). **86–87 Alamy Stock Photo**: Mohamad Haghani. **88 Alamy Stock Photo**: Electra Kay-Smith (cl). **90 Alamy Stock Photo**: Orlando Florin Rosu (c). **92–93 Alamy Stock Photo**: Zoonar GmbH (Background). **93 Alamy Stock Photo**: Steve Vidler (r). **94–95 James Kuether. 94 Alamy Stock Photo**: Dan Barbatala (br). **Dreamstime.com**: Mark Turner (bc). **95 Alamy Stock Photo**: Independent Picture Service (cla). **96 Science Photo Library**: Mikkel Juul Jensen (b). **97 Getty Images**: Corey Ford / Stocktrek Images (ca). **98–99 Science Photo Library**: Mikkel Juul Jensen. **100–101 Getty Images**: Corey Ford / Stocktrek Images. **100 Alamy Stock Photo**: Dylan Garcia Photography (bl). **102 Alamy Stock Photo**: Dpa Picture Alliance Archive (cr). **Dreamstime.com**: Duelunemania (crb). **102–103 Dreamstime.com**: Erllre (t). **103 Alamy Stock Photo**: Nature Picture Library (clb). Avalon: Phil Skinner / Atlanta Journal-Constitution / MCT (crb). **Dreamstime.com**: William Wise (cl). **Science Photo Library**: Roman Uchytel (crb/Hyaenodon horridus). **104 Alamy Stock Photo**: Mark Turner (ca). **104–105 Alamy Stock Photo**: Mark Turner (cra). **105 Alamy Stock Photo**: Kostyantyn Ivanyshen (bl); Stocktrek Images, Inc. (cr). **Dreamstime.com**: Linda Bucklin (bc). **106–107 123RF.com**: Zhudifeng. **107 Dreamstime.com**: Iulianna Est (cla); Peter Wollinga (c). **108 Alamy Stock Photo**: Lou Linwei. **109 Science Photo Library**: Philippe Psaila (ca). **110 Alamy Stock Photo**: Rana Royalty free (cl). **110–111 Dreamstime.com**: Bjornforenius (b). **111 Dorling Kindersley**: Oxford University Museum of Natural History (cl); Natural History Museum, London (cl); Dorset Dinosaur Museum (cr). **Dreamstime.com**: Anetlanda (cb). **113 Alamy Stock Photo**: National Geographic Image Collection (cra). **114 Dorling Kindersley**: Natural History Museum (cra). **Dreamstime.com**: Radomir Tarasov (bl). **iStockphoto.com**: Bobbushphoto (br). **115 Alamy Stock Photo**: James Osmond Photography (br); National Geographic Image Collection (cl); Christopher Jones (c). **Getty Images**: Ben Nelms / Bloomberg (bl). **116 Alamy Stock Photo**: i creative (c). **Getty Images**: Kazuhiro Nogi / AFP (bl). **117 Alamy Stock Photo**: NDK (cr); Martin Shields (ca). **Dreamstime.com**: Jaroslav Moravcik (bl). **118–119 Alamy Stock Photo**: Lou Linwei. **119 Alamy Stock Photo**: GL Archive (cra); North Wind Picture Archives (cr); Oscar Gonzalez / WENN.com (cr). **Dorling Kindersley**: Natural History Museum, London (tc). **120 Alamy Stock Photo**: AB Forces News Collection (cra); imageBROKER (bl). **Getty Images**: STR / AFP (cla). **120–121 Getty Images**: Jean-Marc Giboux / Liaison (bc). **121 Getty Images**: James Leynse / Corbis (t). **Rex by Shutterstock**: Florian Wieser / EPA-EFE (clb). **122 University of Queensland**: Steven W. Salisbury / Anthony Romilio (bl). **122–123 Alamy Stock Photo**: Tom Bean. **123 Dorling Kindersley**: James Kuether (crb). **124 Getty Images**: Emily Willoughby / Stocktrek Images (b). **125 123RF.com**: Andrejs Pidjass / NejroN (tr). **Getty Images**: Sergey Krasovskiy (bl). **Science Photo Library**: Matteis / Look At Sciences (bl). **126–127 Alamy Stock Photo**: Rosanne Tackaberry (cl). **126 Dorling Kindersley**: Natural History Museum, London (br). **Dreamstime.com**: Vaclav Volrab (clb). **127 Alamy Stock Photo**: www.pqpictures.co.uk (clb). **Dorling Kindersley**: Dorset Dinosaur Museum (cla). **iStockphoto.com**: wwing (ca). **128 Science Photo Library**: Pascal Goetgheluck (br); Smithsonian Institute (cl). **129 Alamy Stock Photo**: Corey Ford (c); Panther Media GmbH (cra). **iStockphoto.com**: Hekakoskinen (clb, bc). **Science Photo Library**: Philippe Psaila (ca). **130 123RF.com**: Andrejs Pidjass / NejroN (crb). **Dorling Kindersley**: Natural History Museum, London (bl). **Dreamstime.com**: Janina Kubik (br). **132–133 iStockphoto.com**: OlgaPtashko (Background). **132 Alamy Stock Photo**: Corey Ford (cr); Mohamad Haghani (cl); Rosanne Tackaberry (cla). **133 123RF.com**: Andrejs Pidjass / NejroN (cr). **Dorling Kindersley**: Royal British Columbia Museum, Victoria, Canada (cr). **Science Photo Library**: Dirk Wiersma (cla). **134–135 123RF.com**: Zhudifeng (Background). **Alamy Stock Photo**: Stocktrek Images, Inc. (bc). **134 Alamy Stock Photo**: Mark Turner (cra). **135 123RF.com**: Corey A Ford (cb). **Alamy Stock Photo**: Corey Ford (cra); GL Archive (cr). **137 Alamy Stock Photo**: Mohamad Haghani (br). **141 Dreamstime.com**: Anetlanda (cla). **142 123RF.com**: Oleg Palii (b)

Endpaper images: *Front:* **Alamy Stock Photo**: MasPix

Cover images: *Front:* **123RF.com**: Igor Zhuravlov / ig0rzh / NASA JPL-Caltech (Background); **Dreamstime.com**: Marciomauro; *Back:* **123RF.com**: Igor Zhuravlov / ig0rzh / NASA JPL-Caltech (Background); **Alamy Stock Photo**: Mohamad Haghani tr; **Dorling Kindersley**: Simon Mumford / Colorado Plateau Geosystems Inc. cra; **Dreamstime.com**: Anetlanda clb, Leonello Calvetti c, Sebastian Kaulitzki cla, Mr1805 fcl; *Spine:* **Dorling Kindersley**: Dan Crisp cb, bc

All other images © Dorling Kindersley
For further information see: www.dkimages.com